I0469025

Small Business, Big Profits!!

Creating the Most Profitable Business
Possible Simply & Easily!

By

David Peters

For

The Entrepreneur Skills Institute

All Rights Reserved – 2016 –
The Entrepreneur Skills Institute

Disclaimer

There are many variables when it comes to starting or operating a new business. Types of business can vary as well the owners themselves, the markets in which they operate and the location and design of their business. For this reason and for other reasons too many to list in full, it is not possible to create one master business building process that insures success. Because of this it is up to the reader to determine which aspects of this book, and which parts of the content, make sense for their own business and situation. The writers, publishers and resellers of this book assume no responsibility for the use or application of any or all parts of this publication. That responsibility lies solely with the reader and the reader alone. We also suggest that before making any changes to your business that you consultant with an accountant, attorney and a business consultant.

Contents

Introduction

If you are like me, you want to earn either some extra money from a new or existing business or you want to quit your regular job and have your own business that is capable of supporting you and your family for the rest of your life. For many people, other than health and happiness, that is their greatest dream.

By reading this book I can assume that you are at least thinking about owning or starting your own business. Maybe you already have an established business or looking to grow it or maybe you are in the idea or planning stages. It really doesn't matter where you are right now. You cannot change the past but you can start impacting your future. And that is exactly what this book is going to help you to do.

Before we get started. I want to dispel a few myths for you. You probably are aware of a couple of them but some might surprise you a bit and that's OK.

Because, as you will understand as you get further into this book, sometimes becoming aware of something is all you need to really change your results.

The first myth I want to dispute is that it takes a lot of knowledge and expertise to run your own business. That is simply just not true. There are a lot of people with normal or average intelligence that are operating successful businesses all over the world. You do not have to be a genius or a unique individual to succeed in your own business. If you have the desire and work ethic, you can achieve almost anything in this life. So don't think any of this is above you.

Second, starting and running a successful business is not something that happens with a click of your mouse or by some "auto-pilot" business that you start at 9AM and you retire at 10:15AM with more money than you can imagine. It just doesn't work that way. That is why we didn't call this book "Small Business, Instant Millions". Building a successful long-term business takes time and patience. You can do it, it just will not happen overnight.

Third, and this one is very important for a lot of people, starting your own business does not have to cost you a lot of money. Most businesses today can at least be started online for less than $50 which is within everyone's budget. After all, if you cannot invest $50 then you are going to have a very difficult time financing any kind of business.

So you can get started and once you start generating profits, you can use those profits to finance the growth of your business. So do not let money scare you away.

Fourth, and this is a HUGE one, operating a successful business is no harder than running an unsuccessful one. Most of the activities and tasks are the same whether you sell 5 products or 5,000 products! You still have to create the business, create the products, sell them and deliver them, advertise them and do customer follow-up when necessary. So don't be intimidated by the possibility of your business exploding. Those are good problems to have and they really aren't problems at all.

Our last myth that we want to bust is that starting your own business involves a ton of work, time and commitment. The reality is that starting a business does take work but most of the time you can do things at your own pace and on your own schedule. This is not like having a second 9-5 job. If you start your business online then your website handles most of the customer interaction. You just need to provide support, order processing and customer care and much of that can be automated with certain products. But it will take a certain amount of commitment especially in the early stages.

I guess what I want you to understand is that you can do this.

This is not something only a select few people are capable of doing. For the vast majority of people this is well within their skill sets. They just need to make the commitment and follow things through. We are going to give you a ton of relevant and important knowledge to help you through the process.

But knowledge will only benefit you if you actually use it. So go through the book, read each chapter and learn each concept and action item. But don't stop there. Go out and actually use this information to start or grow your business. While every item might not be relevant or apply to you, the information and ideas behind each item will give you new viewpoints and new appreciation for certain things. So please don't skip any chapter or page because you don't think it applies to you. It's not a really long book and reading it in its entirety will most definitely help you.

Taking the first step is usually the hardest and by purchasing and reading this book you have already done that. There is nothing to be afraid of if you walk into this with your eyes and ears open and do not try to take shortcuts through the process or do things in the hope of getting rich overnight. While that can certainly happen at times, it is not wise to expect it. Plan for long term success and be pleasantly happy when riches come faster than you thought they would!

One last thing before we get started. You might notice as you read through this book that some ideas or material might be repeated a few times. This is not a mistake or us trying to create more pages to make the book look better. Instead it is because the material being repeated applies to more than one concept or because the material is so important that we felt it necessary to repeat it so that it will be remembered better and longer. So if you read something twice or even three times, remember that there is a reason for doing so.

How Entrepreneurs & Business Owners Think

Very often the difference between success and failure lies in the attitudes we have in life. While some people have certain attitudes or approaches that bring them closer to success, others may possess attitudes that hurt their chances of becoming or remaining successful. The interesting part is that people are often totally unaware that their attitudes are standing in the way of their success!

Attitudes are created by a sum of our life experiences and what we were taught by our parents, friends and other influential people in our lives. Environment is so important in our early years because how we witness other people handle or react to certain situations and we pick clues and instruction from those experiences. We also respond to the input of others as we grow up. We are praised for doing things right and corrected when we do things wrong in the eyes of others.

We also develop our own set of values and morals that help guide us through life. These are the things that help us figure out right from wrong and good from bad. Though many times people might say that morals and values have no place in business and that they limit a person's effectiveness, I completely disagree. In fact, I feel exactly the opposite.

Our entire mind contains behavioral pattern for everything we do in life. For the sake of this book, we are going to discuss those feelings, viewpoints and emotions that pertain to our careers and our businesses. But despite this, keep in mind that it is the sum of ALL out feelings, emotions and experiences, whether they pertain to our business or not, that define who we are and how we go through life. So do not discount the value in anything you feel or in what might register a special value or emotion within you. After all, there is more to life than just your career or your business.

Here are some of the factors that will help you become more successful in your business and in life:

Develop a Can-Do Attitude

The world is full of people who can tell you what won't work or tell you what cannot be done. The world is also full of people who make excuses or look for an easy way out. But successful people and successful business owners almost always have a "can do" attitude about them.

By that I mean they look at a situation or a problem and they expect to find a solution. They look hard for a solution. They pursue ideas, eliminate those things that will not work and they keep at it until they find the perfect solution or at least close to it. They look for solutions not excuses.

Even when something appears to be all right as is they look for ways to make it better. They look to see how something can be improved or made cheaper or any number of other improvements. They just believe that everything can be done until they prove to themselves that it can't. This is how businesses and products are started and grown. Not by accepting limitations or excuses but instead by expecting solutions to be found and ideas to be tested.

Take Responsibility for What You Do

There are two kinds of people in this world. People who take responsibility for their lives and the things that happen in it and those people who always look to blame others or look for excuses as to why they were not responsible. Successful businesses are usually run by people that take responsibility for their actions, decisions and behavior.

The reason why it is so important to take responsibility for your actions and what happens as a result of those actions is that we learn from those things and we become better, more accurate, more productive and much wiser in the process. If we always look to blame others, we never really learn from the things we do because we are always telling ourselves it was someone else's fault.

As a business owner, we want to feel that we are in control over our business and what happens each day in that business. We want to understand our success and our failures so that we will be better able to act and make the right decisions next time. When we blame everyone else, we never take corrective action or learn different responses.

Owners of successful businesses are those people who are able to quickly understand changes in the marketplace and make split second decisions that enable their business to stay at the forefront of their industry or marketplace. They do this because they understand that they are in control over how well or poorly their business does and not anyone else.

Once you understand this and start believing it you will discover a whole other level of empowerment and strength.

Knowing that you control your destiny, or at least a large part of it will help you design the best business, operate it in the best manner possible and experience a higher and more prolonged period of success.

Learn from Your Failures or Mistakes

Successful business owners understand what work and what doesn't won't for their businesses. They learn from their successes and their failures. Sometimes what they learn from failure is even more important than what they learn from their successes. And they understand that.

Successful business owners understand that mistakes will be made. It is not a question of whether or not a mistake will be made but instead when it will be made. But it is how we handle those mistakes when they happen that can make all the difference in the world to the person and their business.

Making mistakes is one thing but making the same mistakes over and over again is something else entirely. This happens when we do not take the time to dissect things and learn what happened and why it happened. Without this knowledge we will continue to do the same things the same way and get the same results.

Successful business owners will break down everything that they do and find out what worked really well, what kind of worked and what didn't work well at all. Then they will make adjustments or take new approaches that will bring them the results they need for their business.

This is precisely how businesses grow. They grow by constantly reinventing themselves and discovering what no longer is working well or producing the best results and they make changes. Sometimes these changes are small and sometimes they are huge. But regardless of the size of those changes they all have one thing in common. They needed to be made so that the business could grow.

So the next time something goes wrong or doesn't produce the results you expected or needed, break things down and figure out why. You just might discover one little tiny thing that once corrected, will take your business to the next level or even further.

Be Open to Learning New Things

We all have different strengths and weaknesses as well as different kinds or types of skills. Because of this there is often the opportunity to learn something from anyone you might run into in life. Whether that person is the CEO of the company to the person who cleans the restrooms, you might be able to learn something from them.

Successful business owners understand that there are many skills that are required to start and operate a successful business. This entire skill set is not usually present in just one person but in several, at least in the beginning. Smart businessmen understand that they can learn from everyone they come in contact with. From a stock clerk to a vendor rep to the person who brings the cart in from the parking lot, they all have their expertise.

Smart business owners tap into that individual expertise to increase their awareness about every aspect of their business. They understand that the guy who drives the forklift in the warehouse just might know a bit more about the warehouse than he does. He might realize that there are no better resources for what customers like than the customers themselves.

Smart and successful businessmen or women do not place themselves higher above everyone or feel or act superior to others either. Instead they try to work with people and understand what they do, why they do it and they also ask questions and listen to the answers. Successful business men understand that this is the only way to stay ahead in the marketplace these days because everyone is moving so very fast.

Separate Emotions from Business

Successful business owners realize that they need to provide the products and services that their customers want. Not the ones that the business owner likes but what the customers like. Sometimes the two do not align with each other. Sometimes we put our own opinions ahead of the customer and that always leads to problems.

Smart businessmen understand the need to be able to step back and look at thing objectively. They understand that it is better to stop doing something wrong now rather than later. They understand the faster we identify a problem and solve it the less time and money we will lose in the process. But sometimes this is not that easy. Sometimes we just get too close to something to see and react objectively.

For example, let's say we had an idea for a product and we are in the middle or designing it and marketing it. But the initial marketing tests show that nobody wants this, nobody likes it and everyone thinks it is too heavy, too costly and too difficult to use. In other words, this product is a dud. A real dud.

But because we are so invested in this product, because it is our own idea, because it represents us and our abilities and creative energy, sometimes we think we are right and everyone else is wrong.

Successful businesses make their decisions based on fact and research not their own individual emotions or opinions. This enables them to find and produce or provide the products that the customers want and buy not what we think is best.

Truly Understand People

Successful businesses understand their customers and know what their customers want. They match up their customers with the right products at the right time and at the right place. This does not happen by accident. It happens because successful business listen to their customers, do a lot of investigation and are dedicated more to their customers than anything else.

Successful businesses are responsive to their customer's needs. They strive to become a one-stop resource for everything the customer needs that is related to their type of business. They make great efforts to understand how their customers think, why they need what they need and what they are looking for in terms of products and services.

Then they match those needs with the best products and the best support and service they can possibly deliver. The result is a business that is focused on the customer and giving the customer the most of what they need and want from that business.

This gives the customer every reason to come back in the future and few, if any, reasons for them to even consider looking elsewhere.

Be Able to Make Decisions

Businesses are not stagnant or fixed entities. Successful business grow and change over time. They change their products and services. They change their business structure and their policies. They monitor their competition and try to always stay at least one step ahead of everyone else. In other words, they are always changing so they can be seen as the best choice in the neighbor or industry.

Show me a business that is still operating the same way it did 30 years ago and I will show you a business that is either struggling or out of business. If you stay the way you are while everyone else moves forward, you are falling behind compared to everyone else. That is why we must embrace change and not fight it or hide from it.

But change requires decisions and evaluations and risks. Some people are good at taking risks and making choices while others are scared stiff to do those same things. Successful business know how to make those choices and how to go about making those choices easier for everyone.

Successful people make informed decisions after doing their investigation or analysis and when they have the information they need they do not wait or stall, they spring ahead and they take action. They do what needs to be done, when it needs to be done and they make those changes at the right time and for the right reasons. This is not guesswork or clinging to a dream. It is following the business, doing the research and making informed decisions.

Never Be Really Satisfied

Smart businesses realize that every day their competition is looking at how they can become better and more desirable in the eyes of the customer. They realize that every time they do something to make their business better the competition tries to do even more. In other words, everyone is constantly looking for ways to give the customer more so they can steal customers away from the competition.

This is precisely why the successful business owner is never really satisfied. They might be pleased with the way their business is performing and they might not be beating themselves up over little things or no consequence but they aren't accepting of things remaining the way they are either.

Successful businesses are always looking for ways to improve their products and services and to find additional ways to give their customers more so that they keep coming back in the future.

They understand that what might be great today is not going to be good enough tomorrow if they do not keep their eyes and ears open.

Successful businesses push the envelope. They demand more of their business on behalf of the customer so that the customer never has a reason to even look anywhere else. If they can find a way to make something better, they will find it. If they can make something cheaper, they will make it cheaper.

Successful businesses will do all of this BEFORE they have to. They won't be forced to do something because they are already losing customers or sales. Instead, they will stay ahead of the curve by making those changes pro-actively because they have been searching for those same changes all along.

These are examples of some of the most common methods of thinking and approaches of successful entrepreneurs and business owners. There are more but focusing on the ones in this chapter should give you a pretty good start on shaping your new approaches and attitudes when it comes to you and your business.

As you go through the rest of this book you will see how these thoughts and attitudes mesh with the rest of the material in this book. You will easily see how easy making some changes is going to be when you train yourself to think and act like a successful business owner.

Skills Business Owners Need

If you want to operate a successful business, there are certain skills you will either need to possess yourself or bring in partners or hire people that possess the skills you are missing or are not your strengths. When you really get down to it, the wide variety of skills needed to create and sustain a successful business are very significant.

You should also understand that we all possess a lot of skills but in varying levels. We might be great at product design but weak in marketing. We might be very good at sales but not very good at financial matter. We might have the ability to handle things in the present but not very good at forecasting what is likely to happen in the future.

Because no one could possibly be expected to be great, or even good, at everything, it is important that we have a realistic view of our skills and proficiency with each one. We might know enough to get by or to get our business to one level but need help to get to the next level. So not only understanding what our individual skills are, we must also understand our limitations.

Here are a several of the skills that most business owners really need to create a successful long-term business:

Financial Skills

The basis of any successful business is a strong and stable financial base. The business always needs to be able to have the funds and resources available to pay bills, handle unexpected expenses, provide capital for future programs or projects, pay salaries and take care of the day to day needs of the business.

These skills are important when it comes to managing these finances especially in the beginning when resources are likely to be at their lowest. Being able to create a budget and stick to it and keep the business strong and financially stable is at the heart of every successful business.

Understanding money and other financial details such as taxes and the real cost of expansion and other expenditures is critical for every successful business. Too many great businesses found themselves out of business because of too rapid expansion or not enough resources.

Organizational Skills

If you are the person who can never find their car keys or whose home is a mess with stuff strewn all over the place and if all your bills, papers and receipts are in one giant box in the closet then you might have a difficult time operating your own business without help.

Running a business means making sure that everything, and I mean everything, is done properly and on time. You cannot forget to file tax returns or pay an employee or a vendor. You cannot lose a bill and expect no consequences. You cannot miss an advertising deadline and miss a month of advertising.

If you were to sit down and write down a complete list of everything a business owner must do on a daily, weekly and monthly basis, you would probably be shocked at the list you would come up with. But when everything is done in an organized manner, the list is more than doable and is usually fairly easy to get done.

But when you have to search for every piece of paper or remember at the last minute that something needs to get done stress levels fly off the charts and the business will ultimately suffer. Failure to pay bills and taxes on time can result in high interest charges and low credit rating which will make getting new money more difficult and more expensive.

If you are not an organized person, either learn to become more organized or strongly consider bringing in a partner or hiring an employee who has strong organizational skills. Next to financial skills most people will find this skill set the most important one when it comes to operating a successful business.

Customer Service Skills

It is amazing how many business owners do not have a clue about what their customers need, want or expect from their business. They make decisions based on their own needs, wants, desires and self-interests and not based on what the customers want. Then, when problems arise, they are not trained or aware of the best ways to resolve problems and retain customers.

Customer service training is important because it allows the business owner to better understand the role of the customer and their true value to the business. This value is often many times what the business owner thinks it is.

This is important because certain decisions are based on real customer value and when that value is artificially made lower in the mind of the owner problems can quickly result.

Plus, having customers that return every week, month or year to your business is what makes your business successful. Very few businesses can survive, let alone thrive, on having to bring in new customers every single day because current customers are leaving for other businesses. Every successful business has a core group of loyal and satisfied customers that come back on a regular basis PLUS new customers that advertising brings through the doors. The combination of both of these groups of customer is what makes it possible for the business to grow or expand.

Understanding of the Customer Base

If you look at the most successful and long standing businesses you will quickly see that the best businesses are the businesses that know their customers and provide their customers with more of what they need and want than anyone else. Sometimes customers will even pay a premium price to get that kind of treatment.

This does not occur by accident but instead by the business owners, and the rest of the staff, constantly looking at what their customers are looking for and what kind of needs or problems those customers might have.

Then, after understanding this, they are constantly looking for those products and services that represent the best fit for their customers.

This is important because at the same time they are running their business other business owners are trying to figure out ways to give customers more if they purchase from their businesses. The businesses who understand their customer base the best and keep trying to give them more of what they need or want will be the most successful businesses.

Problem Solving Skills

Even the best planned, designed and operated business will have problems. It is not a matter of if problems will occur but instead when will they occur. Most of the time it is how you handle the problem that determines the outcome of the situation.

There are a lot of people who do not deal with problems very well. They get upset, excited or they outright panic and the result is the outcome is much worse than it should have been or needs to be. But those people who know how to address problem situations are sometimes able to turn that problem into a positive customer experience or a positive outcome.

Even the best products will fail and the best employee will make a mistake.

Even the best intentions often go awry and people will either misinterpret what you said or be in an emotional state where nothing you say will make things go the way you wanted them to. So business owners who have good problem solving skills will stand a much better chance of operating a successful business.

Sometimes problems can have silver linings because whenever a customer has a problem and you resolve it quickly and easily and make the customer happy, they have now seen you at your best and they are likely to be impressed. Of course the exact opposite is true as well so being able to resolve problems fast and properly will help you keep more customers happy for longer periods of time.

Sometimes problems do not involve customers directly as well. You might develop an inventory problem, a problem with a vendor or employee or perhaps a product design uncovers hidden flaws in the product. By knowing what to do to handle the situation early in the process you can minimize the impact to the business and to the customer.

Problems that are left unaddressed for long period of time only get worse. They rarely go away without action. So it is in the best interest of the business and the customer to handle every problem as quickly as you can and with the correct approach and resolution. Anything else is just asking for trouble.

Conflict Resolution Skills

This is an extension of problem solving and it involves the skills we use to calm people down and address situations where there is a conflict between two or more people. There are specific approaches and techniques we use that can help diffuse even the most volatile situations and get people calmed down and ready to talk. If you do not possess this knowledge problems almost automatically become more difficult and take longer to resolve.

Conflict resolution is not difficult to learn and every business owner, from the largest conglomerate down to the small one person business should add these skills to their skill set.

Negotiation Skills

Whether you are trying to sell a product or get the best deal on your rent or for purchasing from a vendor, learning how to negotiate is a critical part of every business. We use these skills almost every day usually without thinking about them very much. But if you want to get the most out of your money and other resources you need to understand the negotiation process.

Graphics Skills

Today we live in a visually driven society and graphics and advertising go hand in hand.

This is even truer if you are operating an internet business where people must rely on a website and where there is no one to explain or "sell" a product to your customer. In these cases eye catching and impelling graphics are critical.

Graphic skills are a unique skill in that we can product graphics that might look good but still lack the emotional grip that other similar graphics will have. Sometimes you cannot even tell by looking at a graphic whether it is a good one or a great one. It is all in the eye of the creator and what appeals to the customer.

These skills are something that a brand new business can sometimes not afford and where the business owner thinks they can save some money by doing it themselves. While this is sometimes true, if you don't have first rate graphics creation skills, at some point you should consider either learning those skills or outsourcing them to a free-lancer or hiring an employee to handle that aspect of the business.

Marketing Skills

Marketing is often a very expensive part of the business. It costs money to find the right customers and bring your products and services in front of their eyes. There are so many ways to create brand awareness and to reach different types of people that it is often difficult for the new or small business owner to understand where to best spend their marketing dollars.

Smart business owners understand it is not as important how many people you reach with your marketing but rather reaching the right people so that more respond to your advertisements and messages. This is where marketing professionals come into play and they can help any business get better results often for less money.

I always recommend that if you do not have these skills to hire them out at first but watch how your money is spent, ask a lot of questions and pick up this market knowledge as you go. After a bit of time you might pick up enough industry or business specific knowledge to be able to take over this part of your business yourself. But as you r business grows and you want to reach more people more effectively, this might be something you want to assign to someone with specific marketing knowledge.

Sales Skills

Every business needs sales. If you do not sell any of your product or service you will not make any money and eventually the business will fail. It is not a difficult thing to understand. If you want to be successful, you are going to have to make sales.

The key is to make sales the right way by giving your customers the right products at the right prices and giving them as much help and assistance as you possible can.

We want to avoid trickery or high pressure sales techniques that leave a bad taste in the mouth of the customer.

Instead we want to create a sales experience where people get what they want or need and they get it at the right price and feel good about their purchase not just when they make it but the next day as well. We accomplish this by creating a first-rate customer experience that hinges around good and ethical sales practices.

We also need to understand that there is a lot of customer interaction that does not result in a sale at that point in time. Customers might come in for advice or information and then go home to think about what to do. If you create a highly positive and supportive experience the customer will be far more likely to return to your business to make their purchase. There are even a few stores that provide such a wonderful customer experience that customers are willing to pay a premium price for what they need.

Understanding of Laws and Statutes

Today we live in a society that is governed by massive amounts of rules, regulations, laws and statute. Ignorance of any or all of these is not an excuse and neither is telling someone that you hired someone to do this and they didn't do it.

It is your business and it is YOUR responsibility to make sure you are doing everything that you need to when it comes to running your business.

Even if you have an accountant and lawyer (which you should!) you still need to understand all of these requirements so that you can make educated decisions and make sure that people representing you or your business are doing everything that they should. As I said just before, ignorance is not a valid excuse.

Plus, understanding all of the requirements enables you to understand the work required and then negotiate the price for providing these services to you. It is always much better to know what exactly is involved before you finalize the deal. Always have knowledge and always use it to your best advantage.

Management Skills

Operating a business, even if it is just one employee requires a certain amount of management skills. The larger and more complex your business is the more employees and management are going to be required. But even if it is just you, you have to be able to manage all the different aspects or parts of your business in order to keep things running smoothly.

Even when you have no employees you might still have vendors and free-lancers and other people who are providing goods or services to your business and these people must be managed as well.

If you already have management experience, consider that a plus. Management experience is usually highly transferrable meaning that the management one people in one area easily translates into how you would manage in your business. There might be minor differences but the theories and approaches are pretty much the same.

Analysis Skills

Running a business usually entails a lot of reports, charts, surveys and the collection of other data. But the data itself usually does not give us a clear indication of how things really are. We have to take that data, study it and understand what it is telling us. We have to be able to analyze it.

Sometimes sales will go down or up for some reason and we are going to want to understand why. If sales fall we need to make corrections to bring them back. If sales increase we want to find out why so we can duplicate whatever caused this to make sales go up even more.

The ability to take raw data and make sense out of it and turn it into accurate conclusions is one skill that will come in very handy. Making the right conclusions and taking the right action will help you get better results in less time using fewer resources. That right there is a recipe for success!

Be Results Driven

I like to be right like everyone else but what I want even more is to get the results I want or need from my business. I want sales to always be going up and expenses to always keep coming down. I want there to be more money left over for me at the end of every month. That is how I view the bottom line success of my business.

To me what I have done to achieve those results are just the steps taken to achieve the results. What matters most to me is that I get the results I expected or wanted out of my efforts. As long as I am honest and fair with my customers and as long I do what is right ethically and morally, I consider myself results driven.

For example, if I create an awesome looking ad that brings in no sales, I am not going to be proud of that advertisement even though it looks great. All I care about is that the thing brought in zero or few sales.

But if a created a really ugly advertisement that brought in 5,000 sales I could care less about how it looked because it made me a boatload of money even though it looked like crap. I don't have to be proud of the way it looks but I can be proud of how well it performed.

Being results driven means doing whatever it takes (within the law and ethics) to get the desired results. It means constantly evaluating what we did or are considering doing to make sure our efforts are getting us the results that we want. If they are, fine, we continue what we have been doing. But if they are not getting us the required results, we need to realize this fast and make corrections.

I believe we should take pride in the results we get and not just the things we did to get those results.

Be Able to Follow-Through

If you are going to own your own business you are going to be responsible for everything that goes on within that business. That means that you are the one who has to make sure things get done and done on time. You cannot do a task 75% of the way through and then stop. You have to follow through on everything to make sure everything gets done.

Depending on the business, there might not be anyone to stand and watch over your shoulder and remind you what needs to be done. Sometimes it is just you and you need to be someone who follows through on what they started so that everything winds up getting done when it needs to get done.

Whenever things remain unfinished the entire business and its future can be brought into question. We need to be organized and we need to be thorough. Nothing can slip through the cracks or be placed to the side because we have better things to do at the time. If that doesn't sound like you, it is time to bring someone like that into your business before it is too late.

Be Able to Look & See What's Ahead

People who can look back and see what happened are fairly common. But someone who is able to see past today and get a fairly good idea what's coming tomorrow have a huge edge over everyone else.

Business is always part present, part past and part future. You look to your past to see what had worked for you back then, you look at the future to see how well your business is operating today and you look to the future to see where you need to take your business then in order to stay competitive.

People who are able to see into the future are usually the trendsetters. By that I mean that they see things first, they act on them first and they are among the first to provide those things to their customers. In other words they get the scoop over everyone else. Because of this they are the only source in town and they make a ton of money before the competition is also offering those same things to their customers.

People who are able to understand the next great thing can be pro-active in their approach instead of scrambling to catch up with everyone else. That is usually a huge advantage in the marketplace and can help you build a wonderful reputation as a cutting edge business.

Well, that has certainly been a lot of pages about the skills and attitudes that business owners should possess. Hopefully you are already ahead of the game when it comes to some things and you can get yourself up to speed on a few other things as well. But if you cannot honestly say that you possess all of these qualities or abilities, do not despair. There are always things you can do to strengthen those weaknesses and improve your overall abilities. But at least beware of them so you can honestly assess your own abilities when it comes to different areas of expertise.

Taking Responsibility

This is one of those approaches or techniques that should not be confined to just business owners or entrepreneurs. It should be something that everyone does every day. However that is not the case and there seem to be more and more people these days looking to blame everyone but themselves for their troubles or problems.

But when it comes to owning or starting a business, there is even more at stake which makes it even more important for business owners to take responsibility for their actions, decisions and their entire business. After all, if they do not take responsibility for their business who will?

There are a lot of parts to the average business and in each of those parts there might be some things that are within our control and other parts that are out of our control.

But the bottom line is that we cannot spend time looking for who is at fault or who to blame.

Instead, we need to assume responsibility for everything that has taken place and own it. Even if it wasn't our fault, we need to take ownership of it.

But why should we take responsibility for anything that was out of our control? The answer to that is an easy one when it comes to owning your own business. We need to take ownership of everything because it is the only way we can take steps to make our businesses profitable now and in the future.

Something different and amazing happens when we take responsibility for something. Our brains come alive, we wake up and we tend to break things down and look at things in detail to find out why things happened the way that they did. We take things more personally and we take things more to heart when we take ownership of them.

Contrast that to the person who is always looking to blame others, or society, or anything else for their problems. When people do that, they do not feel they are to blame or are at fault so they do not bother to really look into something to find out what went wrong. So the end result is that we are no better prepared for the situation when it comes up in the future than we were this time. That can be both scary and deadly to your business!

For example, let's say you create a great product, write and create a great sales copy and hand that off to a marketer to handle the marketing. Sales are very poor and you lose a lot of money on the product launch.

If you take responsibility for the problem you will research why sales tanked. Was it the advertisement? Did you reach the wrong customer group because the marketer used the wrong resources? Was the product something nobody really wanted or had a need for? Was there a better and cheaper alternative for people to purchase instead of your product?

Any one of these, or any combination could ruin the sales for any product. But if you dig down to find out the real reason and then take steps to correct it, you may or may not rescue this product launch but you will be smarter and stronger for the next one. Many times our efforts that we make today will not show any dividends or benefits until tomorrow.

Contrast that to the business owner who claims that anything he or she did, the product design, the sales copy, the advertisement and everything else is perfect because they did it. So they look at whatever was done by other people, in this case the marketing, and they just assume that was done poorly whether it really was or not.

Here is another example that almost anyone can relate to.

A man gains 25 pounds over the last year because he eats nothing but fast food, sugary drinks and ice cream dessert. He doesn't exercise worth a damn and instead blames his weight loss on slow metabolism, genetics, the stores that make the food and society in general for their opinions of overweight people.

Contrast that to the guy who gains 25 pounds and then breaks down his lifestyle and discovers he has eaten far more fast food than he thought, understands he should exercise more as well and also determines that he had both very thin and regular sized people in his family tree so genetics likely isn't the cause either.

The first fellow, the one who blames everyone but himself, is not going to do a damned thing about his weight loss because it isn't his fault. Even if he has a medical condition that really makes it not his fault he will never go to the doctor to get checked out either. So because he feels he did nothing wrong he will change nothing and his weight gain is likely to go higher and higher.

The second fellow, how understand he is at least partially at fault, will cut down on what he eats, make a harder effort to get more exercise and possibly even go to the doctor to make sure there are no conditions at play that could add to or cause his weight gain. The end result is probably some weight loss, better conditioning and hopefully a much better chance for a longer and healthier life.

The key here is to accept responsibility for everything and then take everything apart and break it down into its basic parts. Then look at what you did and consider what you might do differently next time. You might come up with absolutely nothing or you might come up with something. That is the entire point of the process.

Otherwise problems keep on being problems, mistakes keep on happening time after time and we wind up wasting time and resources that could have been used to grow your business and generate more income. Most businesses cannot sustain that kind of management or leadership.

It is easy to accept responsibility for your actions. All that it requires are two basic things. The first, and the most difficult of the two is to convince yourself that you are not perfect and are very capable of making mistakes. For some of us it is very hard for us to admit that to ourselves.

The second thing we need to do is ask ourselves the right question when we start looking at why something did not go as planned. That question is not just "What went wrong?" but also "What could I possibly have done to prevent this from happening?" and "What can I do differently next time to avoid this happening again?"

Those questions will lead us down the path of discovery and keep open the idea that we might have been able to do something better or differently in the future. The phrases of the questions places our role FIRST and make us dismiss our role in the problem before looking to other people. That might appear to be a small distinction but once we start looking at others it is often hard to come back and look at ourselves.

The entire purpose should be to look at what we do first and take responsibility for our actions first and foremost and then move on from there. Take responsibility for everything and then sort things out on an individual basis. Break things down to their smallest parts and then go over each one to see if there were things that could have been differently or better the next time.

The idea is to discover potential problems today before they become major issues in the future. This allows us to adopt a pro-active instead of a reactive approach which is almost always better for everyone concerned. Solving problems now before they are ever noticeable by the customer or end user is what we should always be focused on doing.

Become Grounded
in Your Business

Sometimes the difference between good business and a great one is how well the owner can distance themselves from their emotions while operating their business. I am not talking about being cold and robot like with the customer but rather being able to see things the way they really are without emotions and personal feelings casting doubt or influence on things.

There will be many times in your business when you will have a personal stake or investment in a particular product or service or aspect of your business and because you are so emotionally invested, you will not see certain signs that might be very obvious to others.

We see this all the time in people who think they have the next great product or idea and they dedicate all their time and money in that product only to find out that no one really has a use or need for it. They should have seen this much earlier in the process when sales were poor during testing but instead of recognizing the signs they refused to believe them.

Building a successful business requires accurate thinking and allowing emotions to play an influential role only when they should. For example you can use emotions to show when a product might have an emotional appeal but not use emotions when deciding whether a product that hasn't sold well in years should still be stocked on your shelves or sold on your website.

It also means basing your decisions on hard data and not a gut feeling unless the risk is very low. It is one thing to invest $100 in something that has a huge emotional upside than it is to invest $100,000 just on a gut feeling. The more exposure you have the more data you should require in order to make a decision.

You will probably find yourself using emotions more when dealing with customers. In customer service there is much more "gray area" than there is in other parts of your business. You have to take emotions and customer needs into account when a customer has a problem.

But other areas of your business are much more black and white when it comes to decisions.

When it comes to finances, understanding how much money you have, what expenses you will have and what you can afford to do at any given moment are more rigid and defined for us. It is often as easy as looking at a spreadsheet before you make your decision. You either have the money or you don't. Emotions do not factor into the equation.

But when it comes down to having a limited amount of money to spend and deciding where to best spend it, we have to base our decisions on factual and accurate information. We want to buy the products that sell the best. We want to buy what our customers want not what we want. We need to always be aware of the role the customer plays in our business and respect that role.

Successful businesses are more successful and make larger profits because they constantly provide what their customers need and they do so without exception and they do that constantly and accurately. They do this all of the time and not just some of the time. This happens when the owners or management consistently makes the right decision at the right time.

So while we are not telling you to keep your emotions bottled up or checked at the door, we are telling you that emotions should be a factor in some areas but should not be in other areas. When emotions cloud your ability to see things as they really are then that can present a real problem for you and your business.

But those same emotions can also be instrumental is making and keeping customers happy and satisfied as well. So be a responsive business owner who has both their businesses best interests and their customer's best interest at heart.

That is one great way to grow a successful business!

Be Willing to Do What Others Refuse to Do

Over the years I have worked with people or knew people who thought that they were somehow "above" doing certain tasks in life. It didn't make much difference what those tasks might have been only that for some unknown reason, they felt those tasks were beneath them. So those tasks either never were done or they were done by other people who were willing to do them.

My thoughts, whenever this happened, was that I wonder what would happen if they owned their own business and there was no one around to do those things they refuse to do? What would happen? What they be forced to do the same things they refused before or would they hold firm and still refuse?

If you truly wish to create a successful business then you should also be willing to do the things that other people are not willing to do.

Sometimes this creates amazing opportunities that while not glamorous, can help make you a lot of money. But only if you are willing to look past certain aspects of the tasks at hand.

For example, there are a few businesses in my neighborhood that just go into people's yards once or twice a week and clean up after their dogs or other pets. Now that is dirty work and something that no one really likes to do but as long as people refuse to do it there is an opportunity for those who will.

There are many of these types of jobs or opportunities for businesses out there. In our area we have people who clean gutters, also a messy job, and they do quite well. One gutter cleaning business in my area has been advertising for over 25 years so you know they are making money!

Some people believe that manual labor is somehow beneath them and they are too good to do it and because of this they often either miss out on certain opportunities or fail to even notice them in the first place. But the problems often go beyond that as well.

There are some things in life that need to be done. Whenever we come up against one of those tasks or responsibilities we have a choice. We either pay someone else to do it or we suck it up and do it ourselves no matter how distasteful that might be.

Since something needs to get done, sometimes we have no choice.

If you own a home with a lawn you either have to mow the lawn yourself or pay someone to do it. If your house needs to be painted you either paint it yourself or pay someone to paint it. If you own a car you either pay to get the oil changed or you do it yourself on a Saturday morning. Those are your options and the same things apply to your business.

But there is a third option that pertains to the examples above and to your business.

That third option is that you just refuse to do those things at all. You don't mow the lawn and allow your home to look like a pig sty. You just don't paint the house and eventually it falls into disrepair and starts leaking and falling apart. You continue to use the old oil until your engine eventually seizes up from lack of lubrication. In all of these examples lack of action or attention to important things destroys some of your most valuable assets.

When it comes to your business, not doing those things that need to be done to grow and sustain your business could cause your business to fail. Failing to take care of certain things can also cause you trouble with government agencies as well. Plus, thinking something is beneath you can limit your business from taking advantage of certain opportunities or revenue streams.

We should also mention that this is most often a larger problem in the beginning of a business when there is not a lot of extra money or resources. In the beginning most of the start-up funds go toward infrastructure and inventory or research and development and the owner does things he can do to save money so that more important things are able to take place.

Maybe the business owner cleans the restrooms after closing time so they do not have to hire someone to do that. They can then use that money to buy more product or hire another part-time sales person. Maybe the business gets started providing certain services that are offered just because they bring money through the doors to sustain the business as other parts of it grow.

The point is that successful business owners are not afraid to do the things that other people refuse to do. If they see something that will bring them closer to their goals or that will make their businesses grow faster or better, they will go ahead and do it. They will not be embarrassed or be afraid of what their friends might think of them. They will just see this as the next step in building their business.

Also remind yourself that some of these tasks, while not glamorous, are in high demand.

You do not look down at the cesspool guy when your drains are all backed up and you cannot use your own bathroom! You are very glad to have him and more than willing to pay them!

You do not look down at the guy who is willing to go up on a huge ladder to clean your gutters either. You look at that person as the person who is keeping you off that same ladder because you don't like heights! So the money you pay him is well worth it to you and helps him run a successful business. It is the ultimate win-win outcome!

There are two benefits to looking at everything around you in life with an open mind and in being willing to take on tasks and projects that other people refuse.

First, it uncovers opportunities for you and your business. If there is something out there that people do not like doing, there is an opportunity to create a product or service that will enable people to avoid dealing with it. The more distasteful or inconvenient the problem or issue, the more valuable the product or service will become.

Second, being willing and able to do a few of these things yourself will help you and your business save money. Just like a young married couple will do more around the house because they have little or no money so will the new business owner do things because money is tight at the beginning of every business.

But a lot of these things are just temporary until we find ourselves more established and with more money or after our business has grown a bit and is able to take on more help and more employees. If you were to look back at some of the most successful companies you would probably find an owner who did a bunch of things they didn't enjoy just to get their business going.

Now that their businesses have grown or their careers have advanced, they have the ability to pay other people, maybe even you when you start out, to do those things for them.

Picking Your Niche, Industry or Service

If you are just starting a business, career or are looking to make either more successful, you might be wondering how to go about making the correct choices as to the focus of that business or career. Some might refer to this as picking your niche or industry. This would also apply to a certain extent for the development of products and services as well.

This is one of those areas where there is no set correct answer that will apply to everyone. Picking a business of career focus is a highly personal process that involves several factors. What might be a perfect fit for me might be your version of hell on earth and vice versa.

A successful business or career is going to take a lot of our time and effort to create and develop.

Because of this we should not base our selection on money or just one other factor. Instead several things need to be taken into consideration when you are choosing the type of business you are going to create.

Here are just a few of the main factors you should consider:

Do You Enjoy it or Does it Have Meaning for You?

One mistake many new business owners make is getting into a business just because there is money to be made. While money is always the primary reason people go into business, it should not be the only thing you consider. This is because your business, especially in the planning and early stages, is going to take up a lot of your time and resources.

Because of this you should pick a business that centers on something you truly love and enjoy. Picking something just for the money that you hate or get nothing out of is a sure recipe for failure! Since we all tend to do a better job and stick to something we enjoy for a longer period of time, this is critical when it comes to starting and growing a new business. It also effects our next item as well.

Do You Have the Expertise Required?

It makes no difference what type of business you are in. No matter what type of product or service you sell you have to have a certain level of expertise in that area. The more expertise you have the better able you will be to service your customers and provide them with the best products and services.

While an established business can hire people with this expertise, in the beginning this might not be possible and you are going to have to at least start your business based on your expertise or that of your partners.

Chances are if something is pleasant for you or makes you happy you will spend more time learning and reading about it, practicing it and becoming better and better informed over time.

If you have the expertise required that's great. If you don't have it, try and find a way to get it. If that is not possible in a timely manner, consider another type of business at least for now until you can gain that expertise. Otherwise your business will ultimately suffer.

Is There Enough Potential in It?

It is a sad fact but almost 90% of new businesses either fail or are not profitable! This can happen for a variety of reasons but one of the most common is that there is not a sufficient market or demand for the products and services they sell.

For example, if you are selling walkers and wheelchairs, you would want to live in an area that has a fairly large segment of the population being senior citizens. The more seniors that live in the area the larger your potential customer base might be. If you lived in a town where the average age was 20-25 you would not probably do very well selling walkers and wheelchairs. In that area you would be better off selling exercise equipment or workout clothes.

You should always evaluate the size of the market before making any kind of commitment. This goes for product development as well. Just because something is newer or better does not mean it is going to sell. You can make the very best and least expensive buggy whip but unless you live in a town with a lot of horse drawn buggies you will not do very well.

The larger the market the larger your potential customer base. The more common a problem that your product or service addresses the more people that are likely to have the problem and will at least be interested in your product. There has to be enough potential customers to support your business in order to create a successful business. You should never start a business that requires the starting of a brand new market because that can be very risky. That should only be attempted by larger and more established businesses that are capable of funding such a business.

What is or Will Be Your Competition?

OK, we have looked at the market and found that there should be enough to support a new business in that particular industry or segment. But now we have to look at one more factor and that is going to be what your competition is going to be when you enter that market.

Keep in mind that as a new business, or a business that is still small and looking to grow, that you are going to be the "new kid on the block" and therefore the business that only a handful of people might know about. So in the beginning it is going to be an uphill battle as you try to take sales and customers away from the more established and well known businesses.

You need to evaluate your competition to get an idea of how well you think a new business would be able to compete in that market. If you are a small business trying to compete against several well know big box stores that might be a battle you could never win. But if there are no real competitors, or if the competition has a poor reputation, then this might be something you could do very well against.

But this is something you should know and understand before you start your business. Doing a bit of research now instead of later can save you a lot of time and money in the future.

Remember when we talked about gathering information and analyzing it? This is the perfect example of the value in being able to do just that.

On-Line or Brick & Mortar?

Depending on the type of business you are going to start you might have the choice of creating an online business or a physical retail business commonly referred to as a brick and mortar store. Both have their advantages and disadvantages.

Online websites have the advantage of being relatively inexpensive to set up and get running. They are also faster to set up as well. You can get a website up in less than a day and be making money the same day if everything goes right. Websites also can be seen all over the world so it allows you to reach more people over a larger area.

Brick & Mortar stores are far more costly and take a longer time to get up and running. They also restrict your customer base to the area around your particular location. But they also have the advantage of having a place for your customers to go where they can actually see and touch the products and talk to real human beings. A website does not offer that to their visitors. Websites rely on pictures and maybe a few videos.

Sometimes you will have no choice because the business you choose to start will require a brick and mortar store. On-line auto repair wouldn't work out that well and an on-line dentist wouldn't do well either because you cannot get a tooth filled online! But even with those businesses you would have a brick and mortar store with a website promoting it as well.

Do You Have the Resources?

If you are like most people you are not sitting in your easy chair with an unlimited amount of funds just waiting to be invested in your new business. You are probably sitting there looking at your finances and trying to decide how much you can afford to invest in your new business.

One of the problems that doom many businesses before they ever get started is not having enough money to adequately finance the business through the early stages where profits are not generated from sales. Usually in the start-up phase sales fall below expenses and the owners must funnel money into the business to meet expenses while sales starts to catch up.

So if it is going to cost you $100,000 to get your business open, don't start moving forward if all you have is $100,000. You might need $200,000 to finance it through until sales start producing profits.

If you do not have the money to sustain the business through that point you could lose everything.

So make sure you have a financial advisor and a business consultant who can help guide you through the evaluation process to make sure you are well prepared for what may come. If it means putting off starting the business for another few months while you save a bit more money then that is the smart thing to do. Otherwise you could lose everything because you were under financed.

Choosing Your Business Type

Now that we have an idea of what we want to do and how we want to do it, we need to make sure that we decide on the best type of business for us to open and one once again ask ourselves if this is truly the right choice for us at this point in time.

There are several different types of business that we can have and they all have their own advantages and disadvantages. I strongly suggest that you contact and consult with a lawyer and an accountant to find out which is the best option for you. The information below is designed just to open your eyes a bit to the certain types and should not be used to determine what is best for you.

We are not accountants or lawyers and don't pretend to be. But please read this chapter and then consult with your accountant or lawyer so you do what is best for you. While you can always change your business type later it is almost always cheaper and easier to do things right the first time instead of going back and making changes. But again, your accountant and lawyer can help you decide that as well.

Sole Proprietor

This is a business that is owned and operated by a single person. There are usually no employees involved but that might not always be the case. If you are starting a small business out of your home then most people would choose this type of business. But check with your accountant first.

If your business is going to be a small or part-time business this is usually the way most people start out. But there are issues with this type of business and partnerships that can make them unattractive.

Partnerships

Partnerships are when there is more than one person owning a business. When there is more than one person involved in the business they are set up as partners with each partner owning a specific level of interest in the business.

While sole proprietorships can usually be done without a lawyer or accountant, partnerships and corporations cannot because of the paperwork and legal requirements involved.

LLC (Limited Liability Company)

One thing that can be bad about partnerships and sole proprietor business is that unless you specifically take measure to protect your assets the business and your personal finances are considered as one. What that means is that if you build up debt in your business you will need to pay it out of your personal funds.

Even more important is that if your business should get sued for any reason, the people suing you can go after your home, savings and other assets because they are not protected.

But when you set up an LLC business you have a degree of isolation between personal assets and business assets. There are tax implications and legal forms that have to be filled out and fees to pay but you do get more protection.

Corporation

If your business is going to be a big one of if it makes sense for other reasons, incorporating your business might make sense for you.

Check with your accountant and lawyer about whether this is the right option for you and to find out how much this will cost you to incorporate your business. There are fees and added taxes for corporations as well so be careful and understand what you are getting yourself into.

Franchises

Franchises are establish businesses with an already established business plan and name recognition that you can purchase and operate as your own. But you usually have strict rules and guidelines to follow as well as certain restrictions. Sometimes they make sense and sometimes they don't. I would ALWAYS consult with an accountant and attorney before signing any documents with the franchisor.

In addition, be aware that when you buy into a franchise that there are usually on-going fees that have to be paid according to the level of income that the business makes. These fees can be quite considerable and you should be aware of these fees and how large they might be before making any commitment. Again, at the risk of repeating ourselves, get your lawyer and accountant involved.

Home-Based Business

Home-Based Business get a bad name sometimes because of all the scams currently out there for people who want to earn more money.

So just to get things straight, I am not talking about "businesses" where you fill out surveys, mail letters for people or do data entry. For the purposes of our discussion I will be referring to business where actual legitimate products and services are being sold to other customers.

A lot of people have very successful home-based business and they are able to work their business into their daily lives because they do not have to travel to the office or pay additional rent or hire employees. They can operate their business on their own schedule within certain limitations.

Home-based businesses are the perfect answer for people who want to earn a little or a lot of extra money or even a full-time income. Most of them are easily scalable which means you can take what you are doing and replicate it to increase profits and income.

But you also need to beware because there are all kinds of offers and people out there trying to convince you that becoming the next millionaire is just a mouse click or two away. The reality is that most home-based businesses will not meet the claims of the business opportunity sellers and a lot will never make any money at all. But that can also be because a lot of people buy programs and courses and then never do anything with them.

Because of this, I strongly urge you to do your research, and look at everything very carefully before making any commitment. Do not take the claims or testimonials as truth because a lot of site write their own testimonials. Check everything and do not believe or take anything you read at face value.

As we said the type of business you choose is specific to your own needs and situation. You do not want to create a business that costs you more than it needs to but at the same time you do not want to leave yourself unprotected or create a type of business that will not allow you growth or flexibility in the future.

Because of this we will tell you just one more time to be sure to contact a reputable lawyer and accountant and have them thoroughly check and evaluate any business plan you are thinking of. Get their opinion and then listen to what they say and consider it before taking action. After all, you are paying good money for their advice. You might as well use it!

Designing Your Business

Up to now we have been talking about what to do and think about before you actually start your business. We were in the thinking and evaluation stage and hopefully making the right decisions that would take us to the right business at the right time.

Now it's time to take things one step further.

Our focus now should be focused on building a business that will be customer friendly and contain the right products and services for those same customers. Because if we don't create the right customer experience and if we don't carry the right products, your business will not be nearly as successful as it could have been.

There was a movie many years ago that had the line "If you build it, they will come."

In it, it referred to a farmer building a ball field out in the middle of nowhere. Unfortunately that same line does not work nearly as well if you apply it to starting your own business. If you want to have a very successful business, you not only need to "build it" you have to "build it right" and "build it better."

There are a few things you should understand about your new customer and your new customers. In fact, these are things that EVERY business owner should know and understand. Understanding these will help you shape your new business into a business customers will be able to relate to.

Here are a few things you need to know about your customers:

Customer Loyalty is Very Overstated

Make no mistake about it, there still is some customer loyalty these days but it is nowhere at the level that it used to be. The days of people blindly continuing to purchase at the same place for years are pretty much gone. There are just too many ways to reach people these days and far too many options.

Though you must treat your customers well and give them great value that is often just not enough.

You must continue to design your business around the customer so that the experience they get when buying from you is significantly better than they get anywhere else. Not just a little better but significantly better.

Customers Want Value

In case you hadn't noticed, money is very tight for a lot of people these days. Salaries and raises have not kept up with prices lately and most people are making due with what amounts to less money for getting the same purchases. So prices is a very important factor when it comes to where to purchase.

But you can provide value in other ways as well such as more liberal policies, better warranties, better selection, free delivery or assembly and anything else that has a perceived value to your customer. The best overall value will often be the deciding factor when it comes to where to purchase.

Customers Want Selection

Unless you are talking about a loaf of bread or a quart of milk, most customer like to see a wide selection of products that suit their needs so they can make the decision of which one is the best for them. They usually do not like to have to purchase something because it is the only one you carry. If your selection is limited that might be reason for the customer to go search somewhere else for what they need.

The problem with this is that you never know what else the customer will find when they do go somewhere else. They could very well find more of everything at someplace new!

This means researching and providing the best selection of products, accessories and other components that your customers might want. Naturally you have to balance this with the cost of providing these items and the space they take up on your shelves but always strive to provide the best selection possible.

Customer Want Convenience

Unless it's a rainy day and I am just wandering around the mall looking for something to do, when I go to the store to purchase something I want to get in, get what I need and get out. Most of the time there are several other things that I either have to do or want to do so time is at a premium.

Most customers want to be able to shop where it is convenient to shop. They want someplace easy to get to, they want someplace where it is easy to find what they want when they want it and they want a place where they can take their purchase and pay for it quickly and be on their way.

So as you design your business make your business easy to use. Choose a location that is easy to get to. Layout your store or website so it is easy to find the products the customer is looking for.

Make it easy to pay and include more than one payment option. Create return and service policies that are easy and fair for the customer.

Streamline your return system and all other aspects of your business so that when a customer needs to interact with your business for whatever reason they find it easy and quick to do so. That is far more valuable and important than most people think it is. Just ask a busy customer how important it is to be able to get in and out quickly. Most will say it is very important.

Customers Want to Be Appreciated

Many customers understand that they have options when it comes to where they purchase their products. Because of this many of these customers want to feel that you and your business appreciate the fact that they chose your business and not somewhere else.

Making customers feel appreciated can be accomplished by something as little as saying "Thank you!" when they purchase something or greeting them when they walk through the doors. But you can also say thank you by having a customer friendly atmosphere within your business that is responsive to the needs of your customers.

Helping them with a problem, answering their questions, bending the rules when necessary are all little ways that you can show how much you appreciate your customers.

Each of these little gestures will help make your customers tell their friends, family and co-workers about your business and help grow your business at no cost.

Customers want to be Treated Fairly

Make no mistake about it there are some customers who will expect and demand the moon when it comes to what they want from you and your business. Some of those demands will be outrageous and deserve little thought or attention. But for the most part, our customers just want to feel that they are being treated fairly by those businesses that they purchase from.

It doesn't take a lot of thought to realize that you need to be helpful and friendly during the sales process. Most businesses pay at least some attention to this part of the business. But after the sale has been made and the money has changed hands, this is where the poorly operated businesses differ from the customer focused ones.

Well operated and designed businesses treat the customers well even when there is not a sale involved. They will provide value added benefits to everyone whenever possible and they will assist the customer in finding the right product or resolving their product issues all of this with a smile on their face.

Often times how we treat the customer in a negative situation, such as a product failure or when resolving a problem for a customer, will help either drive a customer away or help you create a customer for life. So create your business to focus on the needs of the customer and produce a customer friendly experience so that the customer feels that they were treated fairly no matter what problem or issue they had.

How to Design a Customer Friendly Business

All of those customer demands or feelings all point towards one common thread. That is the value of producing the finest customer experience possible for every customer. It shouldn't matter what the situation might be or who the customer is dealing with. The experience should be overwhelming positive. Just giving the customer what they expect is not good enough. You must give them more.

At some point every one of your customers bought from someone else before you. For some reason, they decided to purchase from you and your business now. Maybe they were told about you from a friend, maybe they had a falling out or disagreement with the other business or maybe they were just unhappy for some other reason.

None of that really matters why they came over to your business. But what is important is that they can easily go somewhere else if they ever get the feeling that they are unhappy with your business. Once you understand that little nugget or information it is easy to see the value in making your business as customer friendly as possible.

In the planning stages we do this by looking at every part of the business from the both the company and the customer point of view. All rules, policies and procedures must address both the needs of the customer and the business. They cannot be biased towards the business or this will anger the customer. They cannot be biased towards the customer or you might place the future of the business at risk.

Instead everything should be evaluated from both perspectives and changes made to help make things fairer, faster and easier for everyone. If something is very close and could go either way, lean towards the customer point of view. You can always change or modify something in the future if it turns out to have too much of a downside for the business.

You end goal should be to have a business that customers enjoy doing business with. A place they can go where they will find what they need when they need it and always see smiling and helpful faces no matter what the situation might be.

If you look within yourself and think about the places you enjoy going to, you will find that they provide much of the same things to you as you would want to provide to your customers.

Financial Issues or Concerns

One of the most misunderstood and important reasons for business either failing or not living up to their potential involves money and finances. Any business needs proper financial management in order to properly serve its customers and to keep the business in business.

When I say this is often misunderstood I do not mean that people do not think you need money to open or stay in business. Most people do understand this but they do not understand the full picture. There is a lot more to finances than just having enough money to open the doors and smart business owners realize this and understand it.

For some businesses, the money required to open the business is only a fraction of the money that it is going to take to keep the business open and thriving until it can sustain itself through the profits the business generates.

Until that point is reached there has to be outside financing or funds made available to the business in order for it to keep functioning and have the money it needs to pay expenses.

If a business owner does not accurately forecast the amount of money that will be needed to sustain the business until it becomes established then the business will either fail or have its growth inhibited due to financial constraints. This is something many people do not realize when they think about starting a business.

I always advise people who are new or relatively new to the business world to adopt the position of a "clueless informed" which means you find a great accountant and/or lawyer and you lay out your business plans to them and ask for their input and advice. Do not tell them what you want to do, ask them what they think you should do. It is a subtle distinction but an important one.

You want to make sure that you have the financial resources necessary to not only start your business but to see it through the building stages. They will be able to help you because you might not be able to help yourselves no matter how hard you might try. This is because we do not have the necessary expertise at this time to make rational and accurate judgments.

For example, you might think you can have your business generating profits within 3 months and you might hit that but your accountant, through his or her education and experiences, knows that the average time required to generate profits is on average 8 months. With that in mind he will advise you to have at least 8 months' worth of case on hand before you start. 10-12 months might be a safer bet.

This will enable you to continue to do the things that need to be done to grow and establish your business for as long as they need to be done. Using your original estimate of 3 months you would soon run out of money and your business will suffer. Had you had those 8-12 months' worth of finances available to you then your business could continue to grow and thrive every month.

Think about the things that most businesses cut when money gets really tight. The cut advertising which is a death sentence for a new business. They cut inventory which means new customers will have a greater chance of not finding what they need. Last, but certainly not least, they let staff go to save money so customers do not get the service they need when they need it.

All of those things are the very things customers demand when they go into a new business.

But not having the resources to properly staff, furnish and grow your business it will take even longer for your business to show a profit if that day ever comes. Not having adequate capital is the first step on a downward spiral that many businesses never recover from.

Another area of concern and potential problems involve the use of finances during the day to day operation of your business. Sometimes we might have to consider the wisdom of doing certain things due to financial concerns or constraints. One of those things might be trying to expand or grow our business too fast or too much at one time.

Expansion takes money most of the time. Money at the start for the advertising and other costs involved with the expansion. But after that has all been spent and the expansion accomplished, running a larger business usually requires more money on an on-going basis as well.

You may have interest costs on money that you borrowed, increase utility costs on a larger building, increased inventory costs, more employee expenses, higher advertising required to reach more markets, etc. So we need to take all of these into consideration when it comes to planning out any expansion or growth.

The last thing you want to do is create a similar situation like we already discussed where you do not have the money required to sustain your business until it begins to sustain itself. This is another area where your accountant can help guide you and enable you to make an informed decision.

Last but not least, when it comes to finances and your business always remember that just as in life, stuff happens. By that I mean that things might happen that will effect cash flow and the operation of your business. You should always maintain a safe cushion of funds to get you through these times.

Your business might also be a seasonal business or a business that might have slight variations of sales depending on the time of year. That is why you should have more funds on hand, if possible, in the early years of your business until you have a history that lets you know what to expect moving forward. It is always better to have too much money on hand than too little.

The overall financial health of your business is important that helps you grow a strong and stable business that will be around to serve your customers when they need it. Your policies and procedures should be designed to help your business stay strong and financially stable. Keep in mind that everything your policies and procedures address ultimately comes down to how much it costs to run your business.

Whenever you create a policy that gives a customer more, there is a cost to the business for doing that. The money does not magically appear from other areas. So always think about the impact on the business when you make any changes to make sure the business can support those changes.

I cannot stress the importance and value of having a good and experienced accountant who can advise you as you start and grow your business. There are things only they know that can help you create a strong and successful business that will still be around decades from now when your customers need it.

Learn from the Mistakes
& Successes of Others

Operating a successful business is not all that difficult as long as you approach things in a rational and logical manner. That means making decisions based on fact and data and not strictly in emotion although at certain times emotions will play a role. But sometimes even the best thought out plans or actions do not turn out right. When this occurs, and trust me, it will, you need to be able to learn from those mistakes.

But even thought when we learn from our mistakes and we become smarter, stronger and better able to deal with what life throws our way, sometimes those mistakes wind up costing us a lot of time, money and other things that might be difficult, or even impossible, to recover from.

Because of this, I believe an even better approach is to learn from other people's mistake and successes. Learning from what other people have done enables us to learn from mistakes without losing the time or other resources we might have had we done exactly the same things.

For example, if you are thinking about changing your marketing and you were considering a certain marketing company, you should do a bit of research on that company. If you see a lot of complaints or mentions of horrible results, especially in your industry or type of business, you might wish to reconsider that particular option.

Or if another business tried a certain advertising campaign that fell flat on its face, then you might reconsider mounting the same type of campaign yourself. Or at least you would go back and take a neither look at it to try and figure out what that other company did differently so you can avoid the same fate.

While you might think your business or situation is extremely unique, the reality of it is that there are other similar businesses in similar situations and you can learn from what they had done in the past. While the ultimate decisions are still yours, having the benefit of looking back at what worked or didn't work in the past can be extremely helpful.

In order to do this accurately you must be sure to analyze the entire situation including geographical areas, type of products, customer base, size and type of business and several other factors. It is also important that you look at how something was implemented or done so you can identify problems or flaws in that part of the process as well.

Examining the successes and failures of similar people or businesses should always be a part of your investigative process before you take action or make your final decisions. Remember it is much better to allow someone else to make the mistake and incur the losses than you. So take a few moments to investigate what has happened in the past before we go ahead and take action in the future.

Create & Follow
a Business Plan

Just like a car manufacturer would not set out to build a new vehicle without a proven design and manufacturing process, neither can any business be created without a solid and effective business plan. There are just too many things to consider when creating and operating your business to even consider doing it all in your head!

Just stop and consider all the aspects of a standard or "regular" business even that of a one-man or sole proprietor. There are vendor relationships to establish policies to create and maintain, products to evaluate, prices to set, profit margins to determine, insurance to protect your business, procedures to standardize customer treatment.

Then there will be business operations and many, many more things that might otherwise be forgotten or neglected until they start to cause problems for you and your business.

The health and profitability of your business is dependent on all of these things being properly designed and in place before they are actually needed. While they need not be perfect and can be adjusted or redesigned at any time, they must be in existence for your business to function properly.

Imagine trying to set a price for a product without understanding what kind of profit margin your business needs to succeed.

Imagine trying to decide on a certain location or rent when you have no idea how much money your business is likely to generate so you can have the funds to pay that rent.

Imagine trying to provide a uniform level of service to every customer without the rules and policies that are critical for that to happen.

The list goes on and on and on and even the most careful and thoughtful business owner is bound to overlook a few things as they start or grow their business. But fortunately growing a successful business does not require perfection. You can make certain mistakes or errors in judgment and still grow your business. But this only happens when other parts of your business are operating smoothly and efficiently.

And that can only happen with a solid and well thought out business plan.

A business plan is a document that outlines the type of business you have, who is involved in the business, who has what roles or responsibilities in the business and sometimes who shares what percentage of the profits or liabilities.

But a business plan also includes projected earnings, expected profits, procedures for various things such as refunds, approving credit, advertising expenses, product evaluation and handling the various vendor relationships. While your business might have more items added to your business plan, and you probably will, this is the most basic items you should consider.

Some of you might think you can and should do away with this because there is a certain amount of time and expense involved in creating the business plan. You might have to hire someone or maybe you have the skills to do it all yourself. In that case the cost will be less but you will still have to invest the time and effort to create a good plan and then hope that it is complete enough.

But the fact is establishing this business plan at the very beginning will save you a lot of money later.

It might even alert you to the fact that this business will not be likely to generate sufficient amounts of revenue required to keep the business open. Knowing this upfront before considerable expenses are made can save you a ton of time and money by making you aware of this from the start.

While you might be able to construct a great business plan by yourself, if your business is anything less than a small business I would urge you to get an accountant involved. They are experienced in what it actually can cost you to start your business and they might inform you that it will take a lot more than you had figured. Again, this is better to know now rather than when you run out of money and have to shut your business down.

But after you actually start your business, this is where your plan will help you grow your business safely and faster than you might otherwise be capable of doing. This is because the more you understand every aspect of your business the better equipped you will be to make informed decisions that effect that business.

For example, if you know what your income is likely to be over a certain period you can better decide whether or not making a certain purchase or commitment is a wise move. Many successful small businesses have been forced to close because the owners tried to expand too fast or too far and did not have the resources to support that growth.

Imagine the chaos your business might have if you had 4 employees and each one of them handled things their own way because there were no policies and procedures in place to guide them or restrict them. With this situation the same customer could ask the same question to each employee and receive 4 very different answers! And if they come back and speak to a different person they might be told what you were told was wrong!

Successful businesses thrive on providing a uniform level of services regardless of who handle the specific situation. Everyone gets the same refund or return time frame because it is indicated in one of your policies. Everyone gets the same warranty time frame as well.

The delivery process is clear and spelled out so people understand when they will receive their products, how much it will cost them for delivery and what they can expect from the folks who make the deliveries. This way no matter who delivers the product the level of service and the answers customers are given will be the same.

The fact is, without a clear and well organized business plan even the owner of the business might not be consistent with their own responses and policies. Now you might say the owner can do whatever they want because it is their business and you would be 100% right.

But you cannot give one level of service to customer A and a higher level of service to customer B. In many cases this is actually against the law even if done for the right reasons! But another problems is that customer A might know or talk to customer B and when one finds they were treated better by the same business, you can bet that you are going to have at least one angry or at least upset customer!

It is not possible to give you a one size fits all business plan. There are just too many differences between the types of business, the types of products they sell and the location where the business exists.

Because of this, please consider these items as the bare minimum when it comes to creating your own business plan:

Type of Business

What kind of business this is going to be. Will it be a brick and mortar store, an online business or other type of business? Will it be a sole proprietorship or will there be partners involved. Anything that will help establish and define the type of business this is or will be should be specified here.

Scope of Business

This is where you indicate the initial size and scope of your business. Will it be one location or several?

Will you concentrate on business within your town, state or country? How large are you intended your reach to be when it comes to customers? Knowing this now will help you determine employee count and other expenses or requirements that might be incurred in order to reach this level of business.

Structure of Business

How is your business going to be structured? How will sales and profits flow through your business? How will you go about reaching customers and converting those customers into buying customers? If there are multiple employees which employees will be responsible for each task? Even if you have just one employee you can "build out" your company structure as if there were more and create titles for each position. Until other employees are hired you would assume all of their titles since you would be responsible for pretty much everything.

Profit Forecasts

How much do you intend to bring through your bank accounts through this business? What do you think your realistic market share will be initially and after certain periods of time such as 6 months, one year and five years? This will help you decide if the business is viable now as well as help in determining your overall success along the way.

Financial Information

Here is where you outline the expected financial expenses such as rent, advertising, salaries, costs of inventory and other common expenses. You should know these up front to make sure that you have enough money to start your business and also to finance it throughout the time frame where it does not generate enough income on its own to pay for the operation of the business.

Moving forward this is where you would detail expenses for future projects such as adding products or services, financing expansion or growth and for whatever additional expenses your business is likely to see in the years ahead. Your accountant should work with you on this part of your plan or at least review it and make suggestions.

Tax & Government Rules & Regulations

Every business has to play ball with the government and that means paying taxes and abiding by the rules, regulations and policies of government. This can sometimes be difficult because no one comes right out and tells you what you need to do unless you have an attorney or business consultant working with you.

Ignorance of any law or regulation is a valid excuse so you had better know what needs to be done when and make sure it happens.

Otherwise stiff penalties and even the shutting down of your business can occur. It is almost always a good idea to consult with an attorney specializing in your kind of business to help advise you from the beginning. Then, once they tell you what needs to be done, listen to them and make sure it happens. It will be you, not your attorney, who will be held liable.

Rules, Policies, and Procedures

Every business has rules and policies that it creates to help standardize and establish certain parameters within the business. Some of these policies might be customer related such as how long a person has to return a product or how long you warranty your products and services.

These rules, policies and procedures should balance the needs of the customer while also protecting the health of the business. If policies favor the customer more than they should the customer might be very happy but the business might itself unable to continue to stay in business.

It might then be difficult to change things because customers will be used to getting what they had been accustomed to and will see this as a reduction in value. Because of this it is almost always best to establish policies and rules that are fair to both the customer and the business from the very beginning.

Customer Care

How your customers are treated by you and your business is one of the most important parts of your business. In fact, strong arguments could be made that it is the most important part of any business. Customers like to feel appreciated and needed and it is up to your business to make them feel this way.

With competition at the highest levels of any time in history, that means that customers have far more options than they had in the past. Because of this customers will take the time to find businesses to deal with that not only give them the highest value but at the same time make them feel good about doing business with them.

Your business can do this as well if you take the time to create a customer friendly business structure that makes it easy to find the products and services they need but also make it as easy as possible for them to purchase them. The easier and more pleasant you make it to do business with you the more sales you will close and the more profits you will generate.

Legal Requirements

Any good business plan will include ways to satisfy all the legal requirements of doing business in your area.

That means getting the required licenses or certifications, registering and creating the business properly so that all the legal criteria are properly met and that your business conforms to the rules and laws of the state in which business takes place.

This can be a difficult process for someone who does not have the legal background to know what is needed and how to go about it. This is one time where paying a few dollars to get some expert advice can help you avoid paying even more money in penalties and fines later on.

These items are just the basic items of any business plan. Your plan will probable include several more things in order to address your own business situation. Time spent now giving the proper amount of thought to your business in the early or pre-planning stages can save a lot of time and money later on.

This is most definitely not the time or place to skimp on time or money. Do your research, ask a lot of questions and start out with a very basic plan. Then, "flesh it out" with specific items that will help you further define your business. Keep in mind that your business plan is a living and breathing plan that can be changed as needed or as conditions change. It is not etched in stone.

It is primarily a guide to help you set up your business, gauge or measure its growth and condition and make you aware of things that need changing or attending to far earlier in the process where it is easier and cheaper to make those changes.

Solve a Problem or Address a Need

The primary reason for people to purchase products from any business is because those products or services fulfill a need or desire in their lives. Those same problems often solve problems that people want to no longer remain problems. The more problems and the more serious those problems are, the more people are going to be drawn to your products and services.

This really shouldn't be a difficult thing to understand. If you think about any product you have ever bought, you purchased that product for a reason. If you didn't have a reason to buy it you would have saved your money or bought something else. That is just the way human nature is and how our minds work.

You buy a washing machine because it is easier and faster than washing your clothes by hand.

You buy a television so you can watch television or watch your favorite shows with the clearest and best picture.

You buy clothes so you can go out in public without getting arrested or so that you will look really good.

You buy food because you are hungry and want to eat the things that you like. You don't purchase food you don't like because you have no reason to do so.

You hire a cleaning company to clean your house because you hate cleaning it yourself or because your job or business take up too much of your time.

You purchase a watch so you can be on time for appointments and for work.

All of these products were purchased because people either had a problem they wanted to solve or a need that had to be addressed. This ALWAYS lies at the bottom of every purchase. Without a need or problem to address people will never purchase your products or services no matter how low they are priced or how well they perform. People will still need a reason to buy in the first place.

But it appears that some businesses are not aware of this or choose not to follow that particular sales approach.

Sometimes it is because of their business model or because they cater to a highly specialized segment of consumers and addressing the needs is something that is kind of automatic. But for most other businesses, ignoring or not addressing the core need or problem will cause you to miss out on many sales and limited your businesses overall growth and success!

This does not only apply to the products or service that we sell but also to the benefits that our business provides to our customers. Anything that we do better or faster than our competition should be made known to the public as part of being able to solve their problems better or faster than anyone else. If we deliver this message constantly and effectively it will register in the minds of our customers on a very deep level. It will register in their subconscious and it will make your business appear even more valuable to them in the future.

For example, for most people, their time is one of their most prized and protected parts of their life. If your business is designed in such a way that your customer can get in, get what they need and get out faster than anywhere else, that will enable your customers to save more of their time.

But unless you market your business that way they might never realize this.

But if your window has a sign on it or your advertisements include something like "We Value your time as much as we value your own! Come in, get what you need, and get out so you can get on with the rest of your day" will resonate with many of your customers and they will at least come in and give you and your business a chance.

The same goes for having the largest selection to choose from. Let your customers know this and let them know that the days of driving from place to place trying to find what they are looking for and wasting all that time are over. Make them aware that they will have the best chance of finding exactly what they want from you. People do not want to waste time looking around. They want to find what they are looking for at the first stop, not the fourth or fifth.

Market quality in much the same way. Tell your customers that you have quality merchandise that will perform reliably for a long period of time. Products they can trust and a business they can trust as well. Make it known that your business is the place to go for a problem free experience. Don't assume your business is known for selling quality products and services, market it as such and make sure people know. People want to solve their problems for a long period of time. Not create more problems for themselves in the future.

If your business is built and designed around convenience, market it as such. Let people know how convenient it is to get to all your locations. Let them know why it is so easy to do business with you. Make sure they know and understand why you're early, late and weekend hours can make it easier to get what they need on their schedule. This can be a huge incentive for people to shop with you instead of going somewhere else.

As for other aspects of your business and how you should market and portray your business in your marketplace, you are going to have to get to know and understand your customer base and what is important to them. This is where most businesses either go wrong or totally ignore the needs of their customers.

Many business feels that the products themselves are the main things that should address the customer's needs and they are 100% correct in that assumption. But where they go wrong is two-fold.

First, unless you are extremely fortunate to be able to have a monopoly on a certain product or line of products, your customers probably have a few, or even several, places where they can purchase those products either in person or online. So while the products themselves might be very appealing, they can be purchased anywhere and not just in your store or business.

Second, while it is great to have the products and services our customer want and need, they will do us no good if the customers never see them or are exposed to them. Having great products is not enough. We also need reasons for our potential customers to come to us first and foremost instead of going somewhere else. A large percentage of customers will buy at the first place they see what they want. We want that to be YOUR business and not somewhere else.

In order for that to happen we need to first determine what is important to our customers. We need to determine their problems and their needs. Then we have to try and figure out which are the strongest or most pressing needs because those are the most important to the customer. Then we promote and advertise our business as the best solution for those needs.

If your business can address 5 out of the 10 known customer needs then you might have a chance of getting people to give you a chance. If you can address 7 out of 10 you might have a really good shot at growing a great business. But if you can create a business that hits every one of your customer's needs then you have a real winner on your hands!

This is where most businesses fail to either succeed or reach their full potential. They might open their doors and do quite well hitting the 5 out of 10 needs. Some owners might be happy with that and stop right there and make a nice living.

While there is nothing wrong with that if that is what you want, what is going to happen when another business opens that hits 7 out of 10? Your business will be in trouble.

I don't care whether you are planning a business or operating a business that you had started 15 years ago. We must always research our customers to make sure we are giving them as much as we can and addressing all of their needs. Not 5 out of 10 or even 7 out of 10. We must try to hit every single one of those 10 and we must try to do that every day for every customer.

We might not be able to hit all 10 and that is OK as long as we keep trying. We should never be happy or satisfied by being "good enough". That is because being "good enough" is a fleeting situation because there is always going to be someone or some business looking for ways to be better than you to steal your customers away.

Plus, when we constantly strive to give our customers the most of what they want and need, we never give them a legitimate reason to even go elsewhere to see what other businesses might offer them. While customer loyalty is not what it used to be, customers will still tend to shop where they have always shopped until that business gives them a reason to look elsewhere.

But once a customer does look elsewhere, they stand a good shot at leaving their current choice and try out the competition. When that happens the old choice suddenly doesn't look as good as it once did. Since it can cost more than 10 times more to bring a new customer through your doors than it costs to keep an existing customer happy, there is a lot of motivation to always trying to hit all 10 of the customer's needs.

And then, once you do that, make sure to promote and advertise everything that you have to offer your customers so they realize all the reasons to come into your store instead of anywhere else. You might not see a huge influx of customers once you start this kind of approach but over time you will reach and convert more and more customers that would probably have gone somewhere else.

This is the very best and most stable way to grow your business. By giving customers more of what they want and making sure they know about it. So take a look at your business structure, improve what you can offer the customer and then make sure they know what you have to offer.

Always Over Deliver

I once had a boss who was so very proud of the fact that they did everything they said they would for every customer. He was very proud that when a customer left his store that they got pretty much exactly what they expected. While that might be a laudable goal, it really falls short of what any business should strive for. So if you want your business to grow to its full potential and generate the highest amount of profits, you are going to have to do more.

Customers are funny in that if you give them less than they expect they get upset or angry but if you give them what they expect they are usually not impressed or satisfied. Giving people what they expect does not impress people. So therefore meeting a customer's expectations is not something you or your business should set as a goal.

In order for people to remember your business in a positive fashion or be impressed with your business you are going to have to give them more than what they expected.

Sometimes a LOT more. Sometimes you have to almost blow their socks off or impress the heck out of them. Going a little bit overboard will not impress many customers. Going to the extreme might be what it takes.

Now this does not mean that you should go overboard to the extent that it damages the business or places its future in jeopardy. Every decision should take the customer's needs as well as the needs of the business into consideration. There should always be an appropriate balance between the two.

Sometimes, especially early in the life of the business, you might have to pay more or provide more in order to get customers to give your business a try. You might have to charge lower prices, provide more expensive or impressive incentives or bonuses or offer other things to get people to give your business a chance.

This is the time between the start of doing business and before your business has developed a reputation in the marketplace. During this time it might make sense to survive on a lower profit margin just to get established. But this should be part of your business plan and also be done with the advice and approval of your accountant.

Although we talked about this already, the value of a purchase includes a lot more than price. While price is important, depending on the item being sold prices might be number 4 or 5 on the list of important things to consider.

While everyone wants and expects a great deal, that "deal" might include value added extras that have considerable value to the customer but cost very little for the business to provide.

For example, let's say you sell cameras and camera equipment. You offer professional photographers as salesmen to help your customers pick out the best equipment. That is an advantage over the big box stores. But it is also possible that people will come in and get the free advice, decide on which camera they want and then buy it at a discount house or big box store. There is nothing you can do to stop that from happening.

But what if you leveraged the value of those professional salesmen / photographers to offer free classes on how to use their new camera plus free advice on specific photo application such as before you go on vacation so you have the best chance of getting the best pictures.

Or maybe you offer a discount card that gives any customer who purchases a camera 20% off of any purchase in the store over the next year.

You could also sweeten the deal by extending that card for an additional year every year that customer buys more than a certain amount of accessories from you. Most products will have more than a 20% margin anyway so you still will make a profit on every purchase but the card binds them to your business because of the perceived value.

What you want to do is create the very best overall value you possibly can leveraging the special skills, talents and abilities of your business. Creating a value added package that others cannot offer or duplicate will not only bring you more sales but it will help distinguish your business from all the others.

Your overall goal should be to create awe in the eyes of the customer when they realize all they are getting when they make a purchase from your business. From a low price to great service to add-on benefits to after sale service, everything you offer the customer will just create more value in the eyes of the customer and impress them with the treatment they have received.

When you create awe in the eyes of the customer several things happen.

First and foremost they become very impressed with your business and never have a reason to even look elsewhere.

This enables you to keep that customer coming back time and time again. This is as close to recurring revenue that you can get with most products. Having customers come back means that you are generating revenue without spending money on advertising and other expenses needed to bring new customers through the doors.

Second, whenever you treat someone really well or give them a great value, most people cannot wait to tell others about their experience.

If yours is a new business people love telling others about this brand new business I town that gives their customers amazing values. If your is an internet based business you will get more traffic, more likes and mentions on social media and more positive commentary and overall exposure.

So as you start or operate your business do not fall into the traps that some businesses fall into. Do not set prices or structure your business strictly on maximizing profits. While this may get you more money or more income in the beginning, this strategy is very short lived and will soon backfire on you. Creating restrictive practices designed to protect the business at the expense of the customer will help accomplish the same thing.

Always remember that the customer is the lifeblood of your business. Without people to purchase your products and services there would be no profits and therefore no business. So balance the needs of the business with the needs of the customers to create a business that gives the customer more of what they need than anyone else.

If you do that you will be rewarded with a core group of loyal customers that will give you a base of sales and revenue while constantly telling others they know about the experience they had with your business.

It may surprise you to know that there are business who do well every year and expand solely on word of mouth and contented customers. These businesses steadily grow each year without spending a dime on advertising. They do not do this by magic. They just made their business into a business where customers love to buy.

Understanding Your Competition

Whenever you drive a car, you have mirrors to allow you to see what's behind you and what is on either side of your vehicle. These mirrors allow you to know what's going on all around you so you can make the correct decisions for your personal safety and the safety of those in your vehicle and around it. You use these mirrors almost without thinking. But don't you think your business should have something similar to help protect it from everything going on around it?

Many business owners try their best to make their business the very best it can be. After all their business represents their future and their ability to provide for themselves and their family.

In many cases their business also represents one of the largest expenses and possibly debt that they have as well. So it makes sense that we would do everything in our power to make our business the best it can possibly be.

Unfortunately, we often have blinders on when it comes to our business and the world around it. We get so caught up in running our own business that we fail to notice how other businesses are changing around us. Since our business does not exist in a vacuum, changes made to other business usually will either positively or negatively impact our business as well.

Some businesses go to great lengths to understand their customers and while this is also a great thing, it can sometimes fall short of understanding everything that impacts those customers and their decisions regarding where to purchase. With that in mind we want to now discuss the next step in understanding our customers and our marketplace. A step that many business overlook that winds up costing them a lot of potential sales and profits.

That step is keeping tabs on your competition and how they position their business in the marketplace. This is important because until you understand what your competition is doing and how they are doing it you can never understand the impact that your competition is having on your business and your sales.

Smart business owners spend a considerable amount of time studying their competition in a lot of different ways. They personally visit the competition (although not in their business logo clothes!) to personally look at the business, experience their salespeople and examine their rules, policies and procedures.

They will also get an idea of the product selection and pricing strategy.

Some businesses will employ the use of designated "shoppers" who will go in and evaluate the business and report back to the owner. This can be useful because the reports and evaluations are done by several people each of whom has their own opinions and interests. The result is an unbiased view of the competition. Something that might not always be possible if the owner themselves do the evaluation.

Smart business owners always listen to their customers as well. This is important because customers will often mention the competition either to compare pricing in hopes of a price match or to mention something that another business might offer that you do not. Why the customer is telling you these things is not important. But the fact that they are telling you means that somewhere there is a perceived value there.

Business owners will look at the advertisements placed by their competition to see where they are focusing their efforts and which products they are advertising. This can help give insights into what they feel their customers are looking for. This can also indicate a gap in your product offerings that you might want to consider addressing.

The main thing you want to do is to gain as great an understanding as possible about the businesses both online and in your area that you compete with.

This will allow you to structure your business to be better able to compete with them more effectively. But there is one more important reason why this is not only desirable but downright critical for you.

Stop and think for a moment about what the competition is doing regarding your business. They are also looking at your business and trying to see what you are offering your customers so that they can offer the same or hopefully better to their customers. If you are not doing the same you will soon find yourself way behind the other businesses and finding more of your customers moving over to the competition. The only way to stop this is by monitoring all your competitors and always trying to keep one or two steps ahead of them.

Once you fall behind and start losing customers the fight to get them back becomes much more difficult. The time to act is now by learning as much as you can about not just the customer but also your competition. Then you can take steps to keep yourself a head of the pack and not lose a single customer because someone else offers a superior experience or value.

Attracting Customers

Advertising is a great way to bring new customers through the doors or to your website but it has one major downfall. Advertising is very expensive and it can cost you a lot to bring new customers to your business. While advertising is important and while every business should advertise, especially in the beginning, you need to develop other ways of bringing in new customers as well.

Some business owners think that as long as they keep their customers happy they won't have to worry about tomorrow. Well, that attitude is only partially correct. When you keep customers happy, most will come back but some won't and those customers will need to be replaced. That is what advertising is for. To bring in new customers but also replace the ones that no longer use your business.

It is important to understand that every business, no matter how good or even great, is going to lose customers every year no matter what they do. This happens for several reasons and those reason are often out of the control of the business or the business owner.

These customers leave for a number of reasons. They might move from the area, they might not have a need any more for the products or services you sell (such as toys or baby supplies or any age specific product), or in some cases they might pass away. So no matter how good you treat your customers there will always be some that leave for others reasons. These customers must be replaced even just for the business to remain at the size it is now.

So the question is should we try and attract new customers but instead HOW do we attract new customers. We have already referred to advertising but as we already said, that can get very expensive. Because of that we should try and develop different and lower cost ways to attract new customers.

This will not only help us replace those customers who leave naturally but also attract more customers to help our business expand and generate more profits. Often this is the biggest difference between businesses that fail or just get by and the businesses that really thrive and kick everybody else's ass in the process!

Here are a few ways that you can bring customers through your doors at little or no cost:

Word of Mouth

This is the very best way to get more people to come into your business. This is because a personal recommendation or referral is the most relied and trusted way to get people to believe in your business.

Most of us understand that the purpose of advertising is to make the product or the business into the best thing you could ever imagine. We know that the negatives are going to be minimized or not mentioned at all while the positives will be highlighted and sometimes drastically overstated. Because of this we do not trust advertising or the words of a salesman or business owner.

It's like asking a waiter if the steak is good. No way is he going to say no because if he was caught doing that, he probably would be fired. Because of this he might not rave about the steak if he doesn't like it but he is not going to say it is bad. He has an interest in stating otherwise.

But friends and co-workers and other people we trust have a kind of built in trust or honesty factor. If one of them tells you a product or a business is great, you are far more likely to believe them.

That is because they usually do not have anything to gain by lying to you.

Another reason this is the best form of bringing new people into your business is because it is FREE and because these recommendations can easily and quickly go viral. When each customer recommends you to a few people and those people in turn recommend you to more people, this can be a powerful profit generator for your business at no cost!

Social Media

While I am not one of those people who spend hours and hours on Social media every day, I do understand the significance of establishing a presence on all the social media platforms. Having a presence on social media makes it so much easier for people to spread the word about you and your business.

Social media also gives you a way of creating a list of followers that you can communicate with to announce new products, special sales, upcoming events and so on. All at little or no cost to your business. Just mentioning a sale or event on social media can drastically increase the performance of every sale, promotion or event.

Developing a Brand

So many business fail to establish their brand. Instead they push individual products and go from one product to another. While this will help sell each of those products, it does relatively little to help establish the business itself to the marketplace. In order to establish your business in your area or marketplace you must establish and promote your brand as well.

So instead of promoting just the latest product, also promote your business. Promote why your business is the best and let the customer know why they should buy this product from YOU instead of somewhere else. It is not sufficient to convince a customer to buy the product, you must convince them to buy from YOU!

Walk the customer through your business in your advertising, let the customer know why your sales staff is the best, why your after sales support is unequalled and let them know that your business has their best interests and satisfaction at heart. You ultimate goal is to impress a customer that might not need the product you are advertising but develops a liking for your business because of what it offers.

You want to establish your business name and logo with quality and customer satisfaction.

You want people to remember your name and associate it with as many positive things as possible. Think about all the nationally known and respected businesses and you will automatically know most of their names.

Why? Because they have established their brand in the marketplace.

Community Involvement

One of the most effective ways to not only establish your brand but gain more recognition by more people is to get your business involved within the community. Volunteer your products or services to certain events or causes. Sponsor or co-sponsor a charity event. Get your name associated with the good things that are happening within your community.

This helps you accomplish a couple of important things.

First, a lot of people like to help those who help their community. So by providing goods or services or sponsoring an event will drive more people to your store out of appreciation. This will increase customer traffic, orders and profits.

Second, your business will get publicity with more people seeing your log and hearing about your business. This might not make a huge impression now but when they see your logo or go past your business it will seem more familiar and they will have a more favorable opinion of it. This will increase customer traffic.

Third, volunteering and sponsoring sometimes has the end result of getting orders and purchases from the people involved in the event. You might wind up with a contract for future sales or services because of what you did today. It's a kind of "pay it forward" kind of thing that doesn't always end up with an order but sometimes can.

Just make sure you are associated with the right kind of events and causes because your business is likely going to be linked to those events. Keep your participation limited to what is good for the area and helping those people that society usually wishes to help. Stay away from political events that just might polarize your customer base and do more harm than good.

Also, make sure the focus of your activities are for the event or charity involved and not on your business. Do not make your efforts into a sales pitch or you will do more harm than good for your business. Volunteer, give your time and allow other things to happen naturally and at their own pace. If you do this for the right reason the benefits will come to your business eventually. If you rush things nothing good is likely to come of things.

If your business is within a certain niche, try and find events or causes that are related to your particular niche so that you attract the type of people who are far more likely to become a future customer.

For example, if you sell wheelchairs and supplies for the elderly you would concentrate on sponsoring or volunteering in events that attract a lot of our older citizens or their care givers.

Speaking & Writing

Depending on the type of business you have and the products or services you sell you might be able to generate customer flow and sales by writing articles or speaking about these products in local or internet venues. If you have an internet business, then posting on certain forums or other sites related to your business can help establish you as an authority on the products that you sell.

Making sure to include a link to your business when you post or write online or to mention your business when you are speaking or writing for other sources can help bring your business almost instant credibility. This can be very useful when it comes to establishing a brand new or relatively new business.

But always remember that the content in your particles or posts or speaking engagements must never turn the content the article or speech into a sales pitch. Mention your business or include a link to it but always make the focus of the content on the topic or product being discussed.

Recurring Revenue

Some business models, even the most profitable ones, are better than others. One of the most profitable business models are the ones that are designed to bring in revenue over long period of time. By that I mean those businesses that keep their customers coming back on a regular basis to purchase their goods or services.

Products or services that require the customer to keep paying for them on a regular basis are usually referred to as "recurring revenue" products. These are those products that continue to bring in revenue month after month and sometimes year after year. These are the products that help you develop a stable business.

Think about the business that you [purchase from regularly. Many of them use the recurring revenue business model and they use it very well. In this model you can afford to make a bit less on every sale because one sale leads to another and then another one after that. There are many of these business models in everyone's life.

Think about the supermarket where you buy your groceries. Not only will you buy bread, milk and other items today but you will by them every week or so for years! So the store can afford to make less on every order because they know they can depend on your business every week for several years as long as they continue to treat you well.

The gas station where you buy gas for your car or motorcycle knows you will need more gas every week or so and that they can count on their customers coming back for more when they need it. They might also benefit from offering car repairs, a store where you can purchase snacks and lottery tickets or even your morning coffee.

The list can go on and on, clothing stores, dry cleaners, doctor's offices, office supply stores and certain electronics like cell phones which require a monthly service plan are all examples. Most people are not aware that many companies sell printers for less than what they cost to make because they make their profit on the ink they sell not the printer itself!

So what does all this mean to you and your business?

Well, for starters having some kind of recurring revenue products helps your business create a stable base of revenue every month. Though some customers will stop coming back for reason we have discussed earlier, they will be replaced by new customers entering the business. While not all will purchase recurring revenue products, the overall base will remain stable or grow as long as you continue to treat your customers well.

The worst, or I should say most difficult, business model is the one where you draw in and cultivate a customer for just one sale and then you have to start all over again. The cost of doing this is very expensive and also very time consuming. It is like you always have to start all over at the beginning of every month. You have little to build on as your customers are one-shot customers.

But if you have a recurring income revenue stream you will start off the month with a certain amount of business and cash flow that you can always depend on. You can use this to more accurately and safely forecast expenses and make financial decisions about your future.

For example, let's say you are thinking about expanding your business which would mean higher rent, higher employee count and more inventory.

Wouldn't it be a much easier decision if you could look and see that you had recurring revenue coming in every month that would cover those additional expenses? Or would you prefer to have to fight for that increased income each and every month?

Most business owners love the concept of recurring revenue because it helps stabilize the financial health and condition of their business. While the rest of your sales might fluctuate from month to month you can always rely on your recurring revenue to help you limit those fluctuations. Banks and financial institutions love to see recurring or stable revenue month after month as well.

So now that we all see the benefits of having at least some products or services that generate recurring revenue, how do we go about determining which ones are the best and which ones will fit into our business?

Here are a few characteristics of recurring revenue products that you might consider for your business:

Suitability

Whatever products you choose they should fit in well with the rest of your business. This is important because they should match the needs of the people who walk through the doors. If you sell power tools and add women's shampoo as a recurring revenue product, it probably would not sell very well!

Continued Demand Products

If you can find a product that fits in with the rest of your business that people have to purchase on a regular basis that could be a winner for you as a recurring sales opportunity. Just take your business and decide which products have a constant need and that also fit in with the rest of your products.

Subscription Products

If you can figure out a product that people need on a constant basis then create an automatic subscription program where you automatically charge and either deliver or ship out the product with to the customer. This makes it easier on the customer while committing the customer to purchase from you instead of going somewhere else. A hidden bonus is that many customers forget they have these commitments and continue to get and pay for the product until they realize they no longer need or want it. Meanwhile you bring in revenue!

Membership Programs

Sometimes you can get more revenue by charging people a smaller monthly fee for something instead of one large price up-front.

Many educational or training programs are set up in this manner. People pay a monthly fee to access information they want whenever they want. This can wind up with more people singing up because the cost is lower up-front but still wind up paying more because they remained members for longer than they expects.

If yours is a business where you sell knowledge or other products that people might need over time, then a membership program might be a good option for your business.

One classic option is to have a member program where your customer pays a yearly fee to become a member and have access to your products or to receive a certain discount on every purchase. Many of the big box warehouse clubs utilize this model and they do quite well with it!

Service Programs & Contracts

There is a lot of money to be made selling service contract. These are the contract that you sell to people in case their products should require service. If they require service you provide the parts and labor to fix the product at no cost to the customer. But if the product never requires service you keep the cost of the service contract as your profit.

A bit of care and research is necessary to protect your business against undo risk when it comes to selling these contracts.

But many businesses simply sell a third party contract so they get their commission without the risk. This might be something you might want to look at. You might consider these a bit more of an add-on sale but if people have to buy them every year or two, you could make a great deal of revenue selling them.

Maintenance Programs

Almost all kinds of equipment requires some kind of scheduled maintenance. Or at least it is recommended by the manufacturer. If you can sell a maintenance package to the customer then you can be assured revenue over the life of the contract while also tying your customer to your business. Oil changes and brank replacement are perfect examples for vehicles while computer tune-ups and virus protection are perfect examples for home computers.

Regardless of what kind of products and services you sell there are almost always recurring revenue products that you can add to your product offering that will help you increase sales while producing on-going revenue. You might already have some of these products and not even realized it.

If you have some of them, start tracking the revenue they bring in and consider adding more to your product offerings. But if you don't have any, do a bit of research and try to see if you can add a few.

The more often you can keep a customer coming back the more sales and profits you are going to generate.

One last advantage to recurring revenue products is that every time your customers buy anything from your business, or whenever they receive their monthly bill or invoice, this is another time you get their eyes on your business and your sales. You can take advantage of this to get better responses to all your sales and special promotions.

Demographic Marketing

All business advertise to reach the most customers. But the really successful business owners realize that it is not the number of customer that you reach that makes the most difference but instead the number of relevant customers that you reach the really counts.

Advertising is one of the most expensive aspects of many businesses. Most business consider it a necessary evil. We use advertising to bring in new customers and to make existing customers aware of new products or product that we have placed on sale. But regardless of the reasons behind the advertising if we do not reach the right kind of people, we will not get the optimum return on our advertising investment.

I have known a lot of business owners who advertise in certain publications or certain types of media because the cost of using those resources was lower than some of the other places where they could advertise. Their reason was why spend $2,000 on advertising when you can place the same ad to the same number of people for just $500? On the surface you might think that this argument makes sense but there are a few reasons why it is a fool's argument.

First of all, advertising is priced by not only how many people it reaches but the types of people that it reaches. These individual customer characteristics or traits are usually referred to as demographics. By using these demographics you can target your advertising to more of the people who are actually considering your products or are already using them. This almost always results in higher response and ore converted customers.

For example, let's say that I sell surfboard and skateboards. I can advertise in one set of publications and reach 1,000,000 people for $2,500. Or I can advertise to 250,000 for the same $2,500. On the surface it would appear that the latter offer would be 4 times the cost per person than the first offer. So the first offer was much better.

But if you looked at the demographics you might feel differently.

Suppose that the publications you would be advertising in with the first group were all senior citizens magazines. In that case you would be advertising your surfboards to people who, unless they were purchasing for their grandchildren, would have zero use for your products. The end result would be almost a zero percent return on that investment.

But the publications in group 2 would be publications frequented by people aged 21-30 whose interest lie mostly in outside sports and activities and water sports. This group of people would be largely relevant and if your offer and product selection was good you would likely make a lot of sales or at least generate a lot of leads! So even though the cost was 4 times the cost of package A, you would make a lot more profit because of the highly targeted advertising.

Most of the time the more targeted the advertising is the higher the cost. Now if you are in the business of selling a wide range of broadly used and accepted products then untargeted advertising might work well for your business and be much cheaper. But the more refined your niche or customer base is, the more targeted your advertising needs to be.

When it comes to online advertising, this is even more critical because you can pay to reach millions of untargeted people and not close a single sale. Many of the so-called high response advertising packages are misleading and unproductive.

I once did a test on a new source of internet advertising that appears really cheap for what you were supposedly getting. I sent out an offer, the same offer that usually was highly converting, to several million so-called "targeted customers" and received not a single order! So much for that advertising source.

We have already discussed the importance of knowing your customers. But this consists more than knowing what they want or where they live. You are going to need to know how old they are, what they like, where their interests lie and what things they enjoy doing in life.

All of this information is gathered from past purchases, magazine subscriptions, attendance at events, mailing lists they signed up for and a host of other sources all designed to take all of the information and assign that person to the right lists of targeted customers.

All of this is expensive but in the long run, if you can match the right offer with the right customer you can make a lot of money in a shorter period of time. Here are a few reasons why targeted advertising using quality demographics can give you such a higher response than other advertising:

Better Qualified Recipients

By targeting advertising to the people who have a better change of wanting or needing your products, you will get a larger engagement than if you just mass mail or market to the general public. By targeting you can eliminate a lot of people that will likely have little or no use for your products and spend your money reaching the people that do.

Higher Response Rate

When you advertise to the people that have a greater chance of using what you sell, you almost always get a higher response rate to your offers and advertising. Since a high response rate is so important for several reasons, anything we can do to get a high response rate is worth the effort.

Higher Open or Read Rate

People get inundated with all kinds of advertising these days. Far more than they would like. E-Mil in boxes are clogged with crap and our mailboxes are overflowing with mail we don't want and just throw away.

But when you get an e-mail or printed material for something you have an interest in, you are far more likely to get a pair of eyes on it at least to see what it is about. After all, an e-mail that is never opened is worthless. The same for a printed piece that makes it from the mailbox straight into the trash or recycle bin.

Target advertising is far more likely to be at least partially read than non-targeted advertising. You still need a compelling offer to catch the eyes of the customer but at least you will have a chance to catch those eyes because they at least read a little of it and didn't just toss it.

Higher Conversion Rate

It goes to say that if you send an offer to people who are interested in it you are going to close more sales and make more money. Converting readers into buyers still will require the right offer but getting that offer into the hands of the people most likely to respond to it is what we need to do.

So moving forward, make the effort to understand who and what your customers are and then target your advertising accordingly. Take the steps necessary to get your promotions and offers into the hands of the people far more likely to want or need them. It may costs you a few more dollars but it will bring in a lot more sales and revenue if you just put in the effort.

Test, Evaluate, Revise

Have you noticed that sometimes businesses that have been around for years one day just close up their doors and go out of business? Sometimes the reason is clear to see as when more competition comes into the area that they just cannot compete with. Such is the story whenever those big box stores come into town. Then there are businesses who sell items that we now longer need so the demand falls way off. Anyone remember the video stores in the 80's and 90's? That is a perfect example.

But one of the reasons a lot of business that were once successful and profitable often go out of business is that they refuse to change along with the times. Even many business who are still in business are much less successful than they could be because they refuse to change.

It is really easy just to keep on doing what works for your business. After all, if you started a business doing things a certain way and that business has grown into a very successful business, why would you consider changing what has worked so well for you in the past?

You should be receptive to change because as everything around us change, those changes often impact our businesses as well. If we do not stay ahead of those changes, if we do not see what's coming and adapt to it, we might find ourselves too far behind the times to compete effectively.

The good part about this is that we are not usually talking about massive changes. We are talking about changing a small thing here, tweaking something there and making small adjustments designed to make our businesses stronger, more desirable and more profitable. As long as we constantly do this and remain current and productive, a huge or widespread change is not usually required.

Another reason for doing this is that just because something works, it doesn't mean that it is working at its best. Maybe a product that is bringing in $1,000 a month could really be bringing in $10,000 a month if we marketed it differently or made some other change. Our goal should be to make every part of our business as efficient and profitable as we can.

There is a 3 part process that every business should be constantly implementing. This is the test, evaluate and revise method. As named, this is a three step process designed to guide you in the right direction. Here are the three steps and what is involved in each step:

Test

Here is where we determine what part of our business might need to be updated or changed. Then we determine what changes should be made and we implement one of those changes in a test product or part of our market. We do not make a wholesale change because we want to be able to compare what we have now against what we might have if we made the change.

For example, maybe we institute a pricing change in a few chosen markets to see if lower or higher prices will produce more or less profits. We would compare the performance of the test markets against the rest of the business to get an idea if changing the price makes sense.

Or maybe we make a different product available in some locations to see which product sells better. Since shelf space can be extremely valuable, we want to place the products that will sell the most on our shelves whenever we possibly can. So we change to a different product in a few locations and compare those sales against the locations with the older product.

Or, if we have one location we compare sales of the new versus the old products.

The list can go on and on but what we are doing in this stage is creating a test market so we can see on a limited scale how making a certain change will affect our business. Then, after the test is completed and we have some data to look at, we go ahead to step two of the process.

Before we go to step two let me say one more thing about the testing process. As we go through the process we should change just one thing at a time in each area of the business. This is important because we need to understand which changes accomplished which results. If we change two things about a certain product and the result was no change at all, we might never know that one change boosted sales 50% while the other change reduced sales 50%! So change one thing at a time so your results will be valid.

Evaluate

The evaluation phase is where we take the results, or the data, and determine if the changes we made had the desired results or not. Did the changes make things better, worse or did they stay the same? In this phase of the process we are looking for accurate data and not just an opinion to help us arrive at the same conclusion.

Data is important because it takes the guesswork and opinion out of the process. We need data to see the big overall picture and not just what we observed or what we wanted to see. This enables us to make valid decisions that will have a positive effect on our business.

Revise

When something appears to work well, we can either proceed with the change to the rest of the business or determine whether we should make additional changes to further test what we should do.

For example, if we increased the price 5% and it still sold well, we might want to try a 10% increase in other locations and test that to see what effect that has on our sales. Or if we make a change to a rule or procedure, we might want to see if making additional changes might be a good idea as well. This will help us get the most out of making a change and not result in us settling for less than what we could have.

If a change did not get the desired results we have to dig a bit deeper and determine why. We can look at what happened and determine what the next step might be. That could be making a different change or leaving something as it currently stands.

Not everything in your business should be changed or even needs to be changed. But as the world around us changes, and as new products and services are created, what we do in our business needs to change as well. Many businesses fail to keep up with trends and customer needs and those are the businesses that often fail even after many decades of operation.

We should constantly be testing and evaluating the products we sell, the rules and procedures we enforce and how our business stands within the industry. We need to constantly check out what our competition is doing so that we can change our business to make it more customer friendly.

Change is not always difficult and it is not always painful. But change is what is needed to keep our businesses current and responsive to our customers. The key to change is gathering accurate data and having an organized method of procuring that data and then be able to accurately analyze that data once you have it.

Making small changes as they are needed is the best way of keeping your business on the forefront of things and not having to constantly play catch up with your customers and your competition. After all, it is far better to do things in a pro-active manner and on your schedule rather than be forced to react to something faster than you would like to.

Never Be Satisfied

This can be a tough one because it involves the ability to create a balance between being happy with your business while at the same time making it better and more profitable. How you actually approach this concept will have a great deal to do with the type of person you are and how you view your business.

Some business owners are constantly looking for ways to improve their business and are never happy with what they have. They always feel something can be made better, that any amount of sales is not good enough and that there is always something that can be done to bring in more money and more profits. These business owners are exceptionally driven to produce the best results.

Other owners are happy just to have a successful business that generates enough income to allow them to lead the lifestyle they want.

They do not work 200 hours a week and their thoughts are not on business all the time and they are not laser focused on everything that is going on around them. As long as the business is running well, they will enjoy the process.

I guess what I am going to advise is that we blend the two types together to get a business owner who is never totally satisfied and believes that things can always be made better but attempts to do this in moderation. The kind of owner who takes time out to enjoy his or her business and the rest of life while still looking to make their business better.

In other words, we need to create a balance where we attend to our business but also take care of the rest of life as well. We work at our business, we try to make it better but we also spend time and pay attention to our families and other parts of life as well. I guess you could say that we want to be someone who is never complacent but never obsessed either.

Many businesses, once they because successful or profitable, are pretty much left alone to bring in money and stay successful. They continue to function on what has always worked. But in the last chapter we showed you why that doesn't work. We showed you how this could become the death sentence for your business.

The right way to approach running your own business is to always look for ways to make things better. Even something that is working well could possibly be improved. Never be really satisfied with things the way they are. Always have an inquisitive mind that is ready, willing and able to look at every part of your business and try to make it better.

You can do this by coming up with your own ideas "steal" ideas from your competition or other businesses and by reading business and trade journals and improving your business knowledge.

But most important, you can do this by listening to your employees and your customers. These are the people who are right on the front lines on both sides of your business. Listen to the comments they make both good and bad. Any complaint just might be notice that some part of your business can be made better or more customer friendly.

If you hear the same complaint more than once chances are there is something behind that complaint. After all, people don't usually say things just to hear themselves talk. Be open to criticism and take every comment to heart.

You might as far as asking your customers what you could do to make your business better or more customer friendly. Make it easy for them to talk to you. Offer them a coupon or free gift for giving you their opinions.

This is critical because there is one thing most business owners do not realize when it comes to their customers.

That is unless asked most customers will not complain when something goes wrong. Instead, they just leave and go somewhere else and the problem goes unresolved and more customers are effected. By asking customers and soliciting their opinions you can gather far more information and insight about your business.

But do this in a reasonable manner. Do not expect or demand that everything get fixed all at once. Do not work 150 hours a week on your business or expect anyone else to do so either. You need to create a balance in life between your business and everything else. Failure to do this will lead to burn out, fatigue and poor decision making.

Take it slow, never be totally satisfied and always try to make your business better and more customer friendly. But at the same time take the time to enjoy family, friends and the other parts of life so your business complements your life and does not become a burden to you.

Help People Help Themselves

In this chapter I would like to approach a topic we covered earlier in this book but from a different angle. That topic was that all businesses and products exist because there are either needs to fulfill or problems that need to be solved. Successful businesses are the ones that manage to solve or address these problems, faster, easier or better than anyone else.

There are two basic ways to address or solve a problem or need. The first is to take care of the problem yourself such as by providing a service that takes care of the issue. Examples of this might be auto repair, computer repair, home cleaning, home repairs and similar types of services and products. In these examples we provide products and services to take care of the issue with little or no involvement from the customer.

The other way we can help is to provide products and the required expertise or assistance to help the customer take care of the problem themselves. Interestingly enough many of the same examples cited above would also qualify under this heading. You can either repair the vehicle for the customer or sell him the parts and provide the information or expertise to enable them to do the jobs themselves.

There are many of these business in both of these groups and we could call them a hybrid business that helps the customer in several different ways. In fact, the more ways we can help the customer the more popular and desirable our business becomes. The more desirable the business is the more people that will come and do business with it.

The key to this approach revolves all around providing options. The more options we can provide to the customer the more valuable our business will appear to those customers. People like to have options and choices and it is up to us to find as many ways as possible for us to help the customer.

So how do we help the customer's help themselves?

We can do that in several ways. Here are a few of the most common ways we can help our customers resolve their problems and address their needs in the easiest ways possible:

Provide the Products the Customer Needs

Make sure you have the products and services available to your customers to address their most common or urgent need. The more problems you can address and the more services you can provide the better the chance that you will become your customer's first choice instead of number 2 or 3. Remember, choices 2 and 3 lose out more often than not. You want to be number 1!

Provide Top Notch Knowledge & Support

Certain products require specific knowledge both to purchase and to install or use. Have skilled and knowledgeable sales people to help the customer choose the right product or part for their needs. Then, after that has been done have people available who can help or advise the customer on how to install or use the product.

Provide Information Products and Assistance

Many business have printed materials the customer can either be given or download at home with instructions on how to do the most common tasks or how to set up and use the most popular products. These are appreciated by the customers because they have something printed to reference instead of having to remember what the person in the store told them.

Plus, this helps the business as well because the customer can use the printed materials to guide them through and can reference back to them whenever they need. This reduces the amount of phone calls and the time it takes to answer multiple questions from frustrated customers. The end result is a happier customer and a less stressed out support department.

Offer Services for Non Do-It-Yourselfer's

Many people want to purchase something or fix something but have no desire or do not have the skills to do it themselves. But these people are more than willing to pay someone to do it for them. The best businesses offer both options to their customers. They will support the do-it-yourselfer while offering installation or repair service to the ones who would just rather pay to have it done for them.

This is all about options and the ability of a business to provide more solutions to a more diverse customer base. The more options you can provide the more people your business will appeal to. This will help you get to number one faster and easier because your customers appreciate the choices made available to them.

Make it Easy for People to Get What they Want

This is a real easy one. People want to get what they want fast and get out.

They do not want to wait on long lines to get help and then stand on another long line to pay for their purchase. Take advantage of technology to automate some of the easier and less complex questions and reserve the skilled people to answer the tougher questions.

The easier and faster you make it for your customers the more likely they are to come back the next time they need your products and services. Time is one thing that many people seem to never have enough of and they tend to guard that time very closely.

Offer Classes & Instruction

Certain products might require a bit of a learning curve before you really get to know how to use them. Camera and certain tools and software programs come to mind. Offering classes, either free for purchasers or at a reduced price, can enable people to get more enjoyment from their purchase while at the same time developing a more positive impression of you and your business.

These kinds of after sale support and instruction often are the difference makers when it comes time to decide where to purchase. Remember these same items can be bought at a number of locations for pretty much the same price. So it is up to you to provide a difference that your customer can appreciate and value.

The more you help solve a problem or address a particular need and the easier you make the process the more your customers are going to love your business. Plus, at the same time your business will quickly become known as the best resource for products and information in your niche or industry.

This is not rocket science and it is all common sense. It just makes sense to understand that people will go where they feel they get the best value and the best experience. Your goal should be to provide timely and accurate assistance, quality products and services to the widest segment of your customer base as possible.

Easy, Quick & Thrifty

If there ever was a chapter that is fully just down to earth common sense it is this one. Yet despite the common sense aspect of the content, many businesses still fail to consider these 3 important characteristics of their business. While this is bad for their businesses, it is great for your business as you can provide these things to your customers and steal their customers away from them!

Here are 3 of the most important factors that customer use in deciding where to make their purchases:

Easy

People do not want shopping for anything to be a hassle or at all difficult. They want what they want when they want it and they do not want to waste time looking for it.

Because of this there should be an organized manner to how you stock your products so that people can easily figure out where they should go to get what they want.

It also means that accessories should be located with the products so they can be easily found when the purchase is made. Accessories are powerful add-on sales that might easily double the amount of the sale as long as the customers can find them quickly and easily.

Other aspects of easy are longer store hours, easy parking, easy access, short check-out or payment lines and other services such as delivery and set-up when applicable. In short, the easier you can make it for the customer the happier your customers will be.

Quick

People also do not like to waste time or take longer to accomplish something than they think it should take. If a customer has to wait for assistance or stand on a long line to pay for their purchase this might cause them to choose somewhere else to get what they need.

The same goes for access to your business as well. If parking is a real hassle and people have to drive around for 10-15 minutes in the hopes of finding an open parking space, this can cost your customers as well.

Make sure people can come to your business, get what they need and leave in as short of period of time as possible. Your customers will appreciate this.

Thrifty

I read that when it comes to where to purchase price or value sometimes does not break the top 3 things that people consider when choosing where to purchase. But I think those studies do not tell the full story because people want a good price and they want to pay a fair price for what they get.

While there are other factors like free delivery, product selection, support and quality salesmen, price is the bottom line when all is said and done. Some people will pay a premium price for certain benefits and services but some will not. Because of this you need to know your market and understand your customers so that you know what has the highest value for them. Once you know what they value the most you will understand what you have to provide to them.

But if you charge a fair price for what they purchase and you support the customer well that combination is likely to provide good results for your business. But price is different than value so be sure to take both into consideration.

While these items represent an overall general view on what customers are looking for, most other expectations will also break down into one of these three categories. So as you build or design your business, keep these things in mind. Streamline your processes, present your products and services in an organized manner and enable people to get what they want quickly and easily.

If you own an internet business, keep the same principles in mind as you create and design your website. Make navigating your site as intuitive as possible and make it easy to find anything someone might need on your site. The difference with an internet business is that you can go from store to store in seconds without driving. So you had better capture the interest of your customer and get them where they need to go very easily or they might just click somewhere else and look there.

Connecting the Dots

Many businesses either fail or do not live up to their full potential because they do not pay attention to several aspects of the sales process. They fail to realize that getting someone to purchase the product is not as simple as showing them something they need and giving them the price. Often times that is just the tip of the iceberg. If you want to operate at your full potential and generate the most profits, you are going to have to learn how to optimize every aspect of the sales process.

Some salesmen believe that as long as a customer wants or needs something that selling them something is just a matter of finding the product that fits the desire or the need and showing it to them. While this is at least somewhat true, it is merely a high level overview of the sales process. To be at your best and sell up to your full potential you are going to have to go further.

The chief problem when it comes to selling products to customers is that you have to lead them through the entire process every step of the way. You have to point out what the product does, how it does it and why this is the right product for that particular customer and their needs or desires.

This is not a "knock" against our customers, or saying they lack intelligence, but often the customer is not aware of certain things and how they might apply to his or her needs. They might see a problem or need and see a product but not connect that product to that specific need. This can happen for several reasons.

First, we cannot and should not expect our customers to be experts on the products we sell. That is our responsibility. When the customer walks through the door or calls us on the phone we should be able to listen to what they are saying, identify their wants or needs and be able to select the right product for their particular situation. We should not expect our customers to do that for themselves. Some might be able to and that's great but many times the customer will look to us for recommendations.

Second, sometimes the customers know what they need and think a product might be a good fit but not really understand just how the product will handle that need or how well it will handle it.

Sometimes this requires specific knowledge or specialized knowledge that we might have but the average customer will not. Again, this does not mean the customer is stupid or ill informed. It just means they do not have this specific information.

Third, sometimes people have needs but are not sure how to address them. This is especially true when it comes to repairs or technology issues. All the customer knows is the end result but not the root cause. For example their monitor might not turn on by outside of making sure it is plugged in they have no clue whether it is the monitor or the computer. The same holds true for auto repairs and other problems.

While there might very well be other examples or situations where the customer might not understand everything, the fact remains that if we want them to buy we need to lead them step by step through the entire sales process so they can be made aware of everything that is important when it comes to making the right decision. If we give them that information we stand a better chance of closing a sale. If we fail to give them this information they might go elsewhere to look at other products and purchase there instead of from you.

I prefer to view the entire process as a kind of "connect the dots" type of process. This is where you help guide the customer through the process connecting his or her needs with a particular product and showing them piece by piece why this is the best product for them.

It is not enough to show them features of the product because the customer still might not connect the particular feature with their particular need. You need to be able to do that for them.

For example, if you have a couple with several children and they need a washing machine, you might guide them towards a larger model because it holds more clothes. But if you just tell them this is one of our largest models, they might not get the importance of that. But if you tell them "This is one of our larger models which means you will be able to do fewer loads of wash every week which will save you a ton of time and water!" then they will see the benefits of owning one of the larger models.

Features of products are only good when the customer can take that feature and translate it into something that addresses one of more of those needs. If they cannot take a feature and connect it to a need then that feature will have little or no value to them. A good salesmen will understand features and be able to clearly and vividly connect them to customer benefits. When they do this they almost always close more sales and sell more product.

But connecting the dots applies to more than just sales in almost every business. It also applies to designing and structuring your business to make it more customer friendly and easier to deal with. But even after you make your business as customer friendly as you possibly can you still need to make your customers aware of every reason why they should buy from you.

Smart business owner understand that if you offer something your competition doesn't but nobody knows it, then that is not doing your business much, if any, good. Maybe over time existing customers will figure it out when they experience something different first-hand but it will not help you close a sale or bring in new customers.

There was a movie where the premise was "If you build it they will come" but that really doesn't tell the full story when it comes to designing and operating your business. As far as a business is concerned the saying should be "If you build it and tell people about it, they will come."

Once again we come to the "connect the dots" approach when it comes to making your customers aware of why they should purchase from you and not anywhere else. In order to close the sale you want to connect everything your business provides to your customers with benefits for that particular customer.

For example, if a customer appears a little unsure of whether they should make a purchase, you can let them know that your return policy is twice as long and liberal than anywhere else so they will be able to return their purchase should they decide to. Chances are very high that they won't but the added security and peace of mind could very well close the sale for you. But if you don't mention your longer and more liberal policy and your customer is not aware of it, you could lose a sale.

If you want your business to perform at its peak then you have to design a sales and business approach that helps your employees and customers "connect all the dots" between product, business and customer. You must not leave anything to chance or assume that something is well understood by all parties. Any time you assume someone knows something you increase the odds of losing a sale and possibly a customer.

If you have many employees it is a very good idea to hold training sessions and teach every sales and support person the importance of delivering a complete sales experience that helps the customer connect all the dots when it comes from why they should buy from you. The process is not difficult and it doesn't add much time to the overall sales process.

But it will help you close more sales, better serve more customers and generate more profits from your business. There are not all that many things that help generate more profits while at the same time helping improve the service and value that you provide to your customers.

This is one of those things and you should really think hard about the value of this approach and what it can mean for your business and your customers.

Thinking Outside the Box!

Running a successful business takes a rational and well organized mind to make sure everything gets done and gets done well and on time. This is important because if things get lost or forgotten it can have a serious or at least significant impact on how well your business operates.

If an order is not placed on time you could run out or inventory. If customer follow-up is not done in a timely manner it could make an issue worse or possibly result in the permanent loss of a customer. If a commitment made to a vendor or customer is not followed up on this can negatively impact the relationship between them and your business.

But sometimes even having the most organized and rational mindset is not going to be enough to carry your business through to the next level.

This is because there will be times when conventional approaches and conventional thinking is not going to help you resolve a situation. When this happens we are going to have to throw convention to the side and learn to think in unconventional terms. This is sometimes referred to as "thinking outside the box."

Not all situations are going to be the same. Because of this it just makes sense that since no two situations or people are exactly the same it is not possible to construct one universal resolution or action plan that will handle every situation properly, effectively and quickly. If we want to get the best results we have to use the best approach and this often means thinking on our feet and coming up with different and unique actions plans.

I have personally resolved issues by taking unconventional approaches that on the surface might appear to be foolish or ill-advised and I have always had great success doing so. Not because I am a master at unconventional thinking but because I taught myself to think in different ways when it came to my business and my customers. I realized I had to do that because the relationship between the business and the customer is the single most important aspect of the overall success or failure of your business.

If you show me a business that takes care of their customers and whose customers are loyal and very satisfied I will show you a business that has an excellent chance of being around 5, 10, 15 or 50 years down the road. It is a simple concept that somehow manages to escape many business owners. These are the same owners who have rigid rules and policies that do not take the customer relationship into consideration at all.

So the question at this point is not should we think in unconventional terms but instead how can we manage to change the way we think when it comes to our business? This is an important question that really has a simple answer when you get right down to it. You teach yourself to think outside the box by training yourself to look at things from two different points of view and then trying to give as much as you can to both sides.

One view is the view from the customer perspective. We always need to factor in what the customer wants, expects or sometimes even demands. While these demands might not be reasonable or even make sense to us, they do provide an indication of what the customer is thinking and also provide insight into what you can give them to make them happy and turn them into loyal customers. That is the first stage of the process. Listen to the customer, respect and understand their viewpoint and understand what they are looking for and what things have value to them.

Because everyone is different every person will have different things that are important to them. By looking at things from their point of view we can far more accurately know what is important to the other person.

The second view is the view from the perspective of the business. We cannot always give a customer what they want because quite frankly sometimes it just does not make financial sense to do so. Just because a demand is made does not mean that demand is reasonable or has any rationale behind it. We need to balance the demands of the customer against the costs of those demands and what makes sense for the business to do. This is important because the decisions we make today will either help or hinder the ability for the business to be around tomorrow.

The final part of the process is to take both points of view, blend them together and try to come up with resolutions that give both the customer and the business the most of what they want or need. This should not be a win or lose scenario but instead a win-win where both the business and the customer or vendor walk away from the situation feeling content and believing that their needs were considered and respected.

Sometimes we are able to give the customer or vendor more of what they want because they often place a higher value on certain things than it actually costs the business to provide this to them.

For example, if a customer demands a free service call on their appliance because it frequently breaks down and is now out of warranty, that might normally cost the customer $200 but actually cost the business very little because they have a technician on staff and they are already paying him. So the free call is worth a lot more to the customer than it costs the business.

Thinking outside the box might involve including things I like to call "value added extras". These are things that are inexpensive to provide but might have a high perceived value to the other person. We just mentioned one in our example of the free service call. But there are usually many more things we can give our customers or other people that cost us little or nothing but have a huge impact on other people. Utilizing these value added extras can help us resolve problems faster, easier and at substantial savings.

But we can also use these same things to enhance our sales process as well. Including things that have a low cost to deliver but have a perceived high value by the customer can make it much easier for us to close a sale with the customer. It is not always about money when it comes to overall value. Things like free delivery, more generous policies, longer warranties and other benefits can make it far more attractive for a customer to purchase from you than from anyone or anywhere else.

Even changing our operating hours so that we are open earlier or later than anyone else could make it easier for customers to purchase from us. As long as we stay within the law and act ethically and honestly, nothing should be off the table when it comes to thinking about new ideas that might help our business and customers.

The entire objective here is to create a business and attitude that helps provide more of what our customers want and need while at the same time protecting the interests of the business. This helps insure that the business will remain in business and be there in the future when our customers might need it. But at the same time our objective can still be to provide our customers with the most of what they want from our business.

Another reason to learn to think outside the box is that it helps make our business different, unique and sometimes a bit quirky. Most people like different or quirky. They love the little things that have value to them that certain businesses provide. Even something that has a low cost or limited value can make a significant impression on some customers. Everyone is different and we will need to constantly think of new things and evaluate new ideas or concepts.

This is not rocket science and it is not something that is extremely difficult to do or understand.

We need to be able to build a business and operate a business where we combine both conventional and unconventional approaches and policies to make sure we give our customers the most of what they need while still limiting the cost to the business.

Once we open our eyes and look at both sides and both points of view it becomes much easier and simpler to arrive at creative solutions and even come up with unconventional solutions to conventional problems. We should not limit ourselves to things we always had done in the past no matter how well they might have worked for us. Instead we need to always look for ways to give our customers more instead of less and also make them feel needed and appreciated at the same time.

Another reason for learning to think outside the box is that it helps keep our business honest and fresh in the eyes of the customer. Every other business is concentrating on ways to make their business better in the eyes of the same customers you are fighting for. If you keep your eyes on the past you will miss out on the future. Other businesses will soon pass you buy and you will find yourself playing a seemingly never ending battle of catch-up as you try to recover.

At this point we have a choice.

We can continue to do what helped us in the past, which is always a good thing to do because it was what brought us to where we currently are with our business or we can also start trying to think differently, try new things and constantly update our new business so that it is always at the forefront.

Society changes, customers change, and everything else changes along with us as we go through our lives. It just makes sense that we should do everything in our power to make sure our business changes along with it. That is the only way we can create and operate a business that will continue to function at its peak and bring in the highest revenue possible.

Scaling Your Business

Suppose you owned and operated a business that was very successful and profitable. That is the hope and dream of everyone who starts their own business. They want to turn an idea or concept into something that will give them the money they need to live the lifestyle they want to live.

Some people attain this dream as they manage to build their business into a successful business and earn the money that represent the rewards for their efforts. For some business owners that might be enough but in many cases this could be just the beginning or they could wind up selling themselves short and miss out on a lot of profits in the process.

With this in mind, I would like you to at least think if there is a way that you can take what you managed to accomplish and scale it up to the next level.

By scaling your business I mean duplicating your efforts to either create a new business using the same principles or expanding your current business into new locations or different markets. That is referred to as scaling your business.

Take some of your chain restaurants as prime examples. When the McDonald brothers started their burger restaurant they made a good living. But it took another person to see the potential in not operating just one profitable location but a string of them each profitable and each adding to the value and profits of the company. Today McDonalds has thousands of restaurants all over the world based on the original one.

Depending on the type of business you have there might be nothing limiting you from expanding your brick and mortar business into different locations or different markets. If you own an internet business then there certainly is nothing to stop you from using the same approach in building several similar businesses in different niches or markets.

Sometimes a business can be limited in potential by pure logistics. One burger restaurant can sell only so many burgers during meal time. They can handle only so many burgers on the grilles or people on the lines at one time. So no matter how well it runs or how much money it makes, there are limits.

But if you double or triple the number of locations you will greatly expand your capacity and be able to generate more money in less time than staying with just the one restaurant. This is how you take a small business and turn it into a giant business! You take what has proven to work and you bring it into different markets or locations.

I am fairly certain right now that you could name 10 or 20 franchised businesses in your town. These franchises were set up to carry the particular brand into new markets. Each location helps strengthen the brand and give the business more exposure and allows them to reach larger markets.

Another way of scaling a business is to expand the product lines into other similar areas. You might add products and services while sticking very close to the original formula that made your core business successful. After all, we should go with what works and bring that success along with us.

If the market and the type of business allows you might take your business into a larger building where you can provide even more products and services and become the business of choice for more people. This is how the largest businesses first started. They found something that works and they scaled it into something bigger, better and larger.

Now if this interests you it is important to understand that the larger your business becomes the more work it is going to take in order to watch your business and operate it properly and efficiently. If you have multiple locations you are going to have to hire personnel to manage those locations for you and report back to you. It will be more work but done properly it does not have to be the hassle you think it is going to be.

Personally I think the difference between partially successful businesses and their really profitable counterparts is lack of vision. Really successful business owners see what they have to offer and they see ways of expending or growing their business in the future. They see the possibilities in front of them and they are not afraid to act on those ideas and dreams.

This is not to say that every business should expand or be scaled. That is up to the original owner and their needs and dreams. It is perfectly fine to keep your business at a certain size as long as that fits your lifestyle and individual needs. After all it is your business and you should make the call as to what happens with it.

If your business is exactly what you want right now and if it fulfills all your needs and dreams, then by all means leave it as is and work it at its current size.

But if you want to earn more money and have your business grow to what might be its full potential, then think about scaling up what you have already done and see what you can create to make thing bigger, better and more profitable.

Affiliate Marketing

While this term is primarily used to describe internet businesses, I would like to get you to start thinking about being able to grow sales faster in any type of business by leveraging the skills and abilities of others. These folks are sometimes referred to as affiliates because they are not actually employees of your business.

Affiliates are people like you and I who have interests in owning their own business but do not have a product of their own to sell or wish to combine their products with the products of others. You might even want to do this in your business to increase sales and to provide additional options for your customers to purchase.

Affiliate marketing has its own set of advantages and disadvantages and in this chapter we will go over some of these things so you can get a good idea if this is something that might interest you.

Affiliate marketing is not for everyone or for every business but it is something you might wish to consider.

Here are the benefits of Affiliate Marketing:

Able to Reach More People Quickly

When you are just starting, or whenever you wish to expand your markets, using affiliates can give you instant penetration into markets you otherwise might not reach. Affiliates who have websites or know certain people who might be interested in your products can give you an almost instant boost in sales and market coverage.

No Salaries to Pay

Since affiliates get paid when they sell something, you do not have to pay them a salary or provide them with any benefits like you would if you hired full time personnel. There are also no taxes to pay although if you handle the affiliate relationship directly there may be reporting responsibilities involved. But the cost of affiliates are much less than hiring actual employees.

Pay Only When Sales are Made

Since we pay only when a sale is actually made, you only pay for results. You are not paying someone who does a bad job and gets you no sales. If someone makes no sales they get paid no money. It's that simple.

Approving Affiliates

I strongly urge you to utilize a system that allows you to manually approve your affiliates. This way you can look at each affiliate and allow only those you feel comfortable with to be approved to sell your products. While this is not foolproof, it does give you at least one layer of protection when it comes to who sells your products.

Customer List Building

If one of your objectives is to grow a mailing list of customers, affiliate marketing can help you do this very quickly. Then, when your list grows to where you want it to be, you can discontinue the use of affiliates and take over all your marketing.

Pay Once, Use Forever

Once an affiliate is paid for his or her lead and you have the customer's information, you can use that information to make future sales without having to pay the affiliate. So you pay once for the lead and then it is yours. Some businesses find this part of the process more valuable and important than making a profit on the original sale. Sometimes it is so valuable they might even lose money on every affiliate sale and still come out on top because of future profits.

Here are the disadvantages of Affiliate Marketing:

Limited Control Over Advertising

Whenever you allow someone else to market your products, you lose a certain amount of control over how your business and products are represented. While you can be quite clear and specific as far as what you allow, this will not stop someone from misrepresenting your products in order to make more sales and earn more commissions. They might make outrageous claims, state the product can do more than it really can or misrepresent the product in certain ways.

Refunds & Recovering Commissions

Once you pay a commission and then the customer requests a refund, you are going to have to recover that commission and this can sometimes be difficult to do. Some affiliates will refund the commissions while other will ignore the request or even close their accounts so you are "stuck" with paying this out of pocket.

You can address this by delaying commission payments until after the refund period expires but many affiliates want to get paid now for the sales they make and are not happy about waiting 30, 60 or 90 days for payment.

Potential Damage to Your Brand

This is a very real danger with affiliate marketing. Any advertisement or e-mail that mentions your business has the potential to not only bring in sales but also damage your brand. People can outright lie about you and your business and the product to get more sales. Then the customer becomes unhappy, not with the affiliate, but with you and your business. If this happens often enough, it can destroy your reputation and your brand.

Producing too Many Sales

Though this is a good problem to have, it can cause you problems. If you take on an affiliate who generates a ton of sales all at once, you might find yourself in a situation where you cannot fulfill orders. This is why it is often advisable to limit the number of affiliates you take on at any one time until you can forecast the sales that are going to come in from these affiliates. This way you can ramp up production to meet the expected demand so you can fulfill orders in a reasonable time frame.

Reduced Profits Per Sale

Keep in mind that you are going to have to pay a commission on every sale. Depending on the price of your product, these commissions can range from 10% to 75% so make sure your profit margins can sustain this payment or you might wind up losing money on every sale.

If you are careful, and your type of business supports this type of activity, then affiliates might be one avenue to help you increase sales and grow your business. But make sure if you decide to go this route that you put things in place to protect you and your business.

You can ask to approve any e-mails or advertisements in advance but keep in mind that if people wish to cheat or lie they will just send out these bad advertisements anyway. You will always lose at least some degree of control whenever you allow outside people to represent your products.

Though you can always handle all of this yourself, it is advantageous to use an affiliate system to handle this for you. This way if someone complains about a certain affiliate that affiliate can be banned saving your business from using that affiliate in the future. Plus, using a third party affiliate administrator will save you from having to track sales, pay affiliates and take care of tax reporting issues and responsibilities.

Used properly, affiliate marketing can help your business grow and grow quickly. If your business is new it can help establish your business in the marketplace much faster than you could possibly do yourself. Just be careful in choosing your affiliates and monitor their performance and customer comments to make sure people are representing your products properly.

Conclusion

Building a business is not an easy or fast process. Though it is possible to create a successful business by the "seat of your pants" it is almost always better to plan out your business in an organized manner to make sure everything is done right and done on time.

But just because a business is deemed successful because it is turning a profit and earning the owner an income, this does not mean that the business is as good or as profitable as it could be. That is why each of the suggestions, tips and techniques mentioned in this book are so important.

Sometimes it takes no more effort to create and operate a very successful business than it does to create a less successful one. In some cases, it might be easier to run a really successful business because of the reduced stress levels. Because of that we should at least consider making a few changes to our business to not only make it more profitable but at the same time easier to operate.

But regardless of what type of business you own or how profitable it might be, the business is yours and you should run it and design it the way you feel most comfortable doing it. If that means you are going to generate less of a profit, so be it. There are more important things than money in this life anyway.

But I also don't want you using that as an excuse either. Money is important as there are some things in this life that we have to pay for and others that make our lives easier, more fulfilling and more pleasurable. Think about this carefully and make sure you do the right think for yourself, your family and your business.

Other Titles from
The Entrepreneur Skills Institute:

Enhancing Success!

Customer Service – Three
Perspectives

How to Make Money FAST!

For more information about
business and other entrepreneur
subjects, please go to our website
at:

http://www.entrepreneurskillsinstitute.com

www.ingramcontent.com/pod-product-compliance
Lightning Source LLC
Chambersburg PA
CBHW071813200526

45169CB00017B/210